The Cornell Manual for Lifeboatmen, Able Seamen, and Qualified Members of Engine Department

D0974525

The
CORNELL MANUAL
for Lifeboatmen, Able Seamen, and Qualified Members of Engine Department

WILLIAM B. HAYLER,
JOHN M. KEEVER,
and PAUL M. SEILER

CORNELL MARITIME PRESS
Centreville, Maryland

Library of Congress Cataloging-in-Publication Data

Hayler, William B.
    The Cornell manual for lifeboatmen, able seamen, and qualified members of engine department.

    Bibliography:p.
    1.Life-saving—Handbooks, manuals, etc. 2. Lifeboat crew members—Handbooks, manuals, etc. I. Keever, John M. II.Seiler, Paul M. III. Title.
VK1445.H39   1984   363.1′23′81   84-1873
ISBN 0-87033-313-5

Manufactured in the United States of America
First edition, 1984; fifth printing, 2001

CONTENTS

Foreword vii

Acknowledgments ix

Chapter 1. **The Lifeboatman** 3
Station Bills and Muster Lists: 3
Lifeboatman Certification and
  Requirements: 6
Lifeboats: 8
Davits, Winches, Blocks, and Falls: 25
Lifeboat Operations: 32
Inflatable Life Rafts: 41
Survival Capsules: 47
Personal Flotation Devices: 48
Immersion Suits: 48
Global Maritime Distress and Safety
  System (GMDSS): 49
Morse Code: 50
Distress Signals: 50
Landing on a Beach: 53
Rescue of a Person Overboard and
  Survivors in the Water: 56
Helicopter Evacuation: 57
Sample Multiple-Choice Questions for
  Lifeboatman Examination: 58

Chapter 2. **Fire** 75
Elements of Fire and its Control: 75
Fighting a Fire: 82
Safety Devices: 87

Chapter 3. **First Aid and Safe Practices Aboard Ship**   **92**
Cardiopulmonary Resuscitation: 93
Near Drowning: 94
Hypothermia: 95
Management of Wounds and Injuries: 98
Control of Hemorrhage: 98
Management of Shock: 99
Management of Burns: 100
Safe Practices: 102

Chapter 4. **The Able Seaman**   **106**
Subpart 12.05–Able Seaman: 106
Subpart 12.07–General Requirements: 111
Topics to Be Mastered: 113
Anchor and Anchor Chain: 114
Compasses: 115
Buoyage: 117
Steering: 118
Lead Line: 121
Blocks and Tackles: 124
Strength of Fiber and Wire Rope: 125
Marlinespike Seamanship: 128
Pollution: 137
Sample Multiple-Choice Questions
  for the Able Seaman: 139

Chapter 5. **The Qualified Member of the Engine Department**   **154**

References   **167**

Appendix: Coast Guard Regional Examination Centers   **169**

About the Authors   **173**

Foreword

For many years the *Manual for Lifeboatmen, Able Seamen, and Qualified Members of Engine Department, CG-175,* was published by the Coast Guard and was *the* authoritative study guide for the ordinary seaman who was studying for his lifeboatman's or able seaman's examination. It was in handy hip-pocket form and was the seaman's constant companion. Last published in 1972 and little changed since the 1965 edition, it is now out of print and unobtainable.

The authors, in conjunction with Cornell Maritime Press, have succeeded in creating a modern version of this useful booklet and have produced a manual which the seaman can still carry with him. In doing so they have retained portions of the old CG-175 which are still pertinent, have brought it up to date by drawing freely on the *American Merchant Seaman's Manual,* the Maritime Administration's *Marine Fire Prevention, Firefighting and Fire Safety,* other public documents, and their own seagoing and teaching background.

Everyone aboard ship should know the elements of seamanship and be prepared to take his place in the lifeboat crew, in the emergency squad, or in fire fighting. In order to be qualified to be a part of the crew of any American-flag vessel, a man or woman must obtain an endorsement on a Mariner's Document as lifeboatman or able seaman.

A thorough familiarity with the contents of this manual will provide for the merchant seaman not only the means to obtain the desired endorsements, but also a valuable base on which to build further reading and experience. Of perhaps even greater value will be the encouragement, in the process, of practices of safety at sea.

George W. Jahn
Rear Admiral, U.S. Maritime Service
Master, S.S. *Jeremiah O'Brien*
1944 Normandy 1994

Acknowledgments

Updating the old *Lifeboatman's Manual* (CG-175) and keeping the *Cornell Manual* current has required the assistance of many individuals and organizations in the San Francisco Bay area and elsewhere in the country. If the maritime community were not the closely knit and loyal organization that it is, our task would have been far more difficult. In particular we acknowledge our debt to our colleagues at the California Maritime Academy: Mr. Louis C. Jacobi, who wrote the "First Aid" section; Mr. Marty Gipson and Midshipman Gini Gatejene, who have drawn many of the sketches which accompany the text; and Midshipman Brian Goldman for his photographs. Additionally, we thank Captain Sam Shaw, Captain Dave Sears, Captain Bob Stewart, Professor Brian Law, and Ms. Harriet Millett for lending a hand.

Of the many individuals and firms who have lent their assistance, we particularly wish to thank Mr. Charles Regal, Matson Navigation Company; Mr. William F. Schill, Chevron Shipping Company; Mr. William Martin, RFD Elliot Inc; Mr. Bruce Seaton, Defense Mapping Agency; Ms. Victoria Darnell, John Sabella & Associates, Inc.; Mr. Dean Cooper, Akron Brass Co.; Captain Joe Murphy, Massachusetts Maritime Academy; and LCDR Robert E. Davila, USCG, Marine Safety Office, San Francisco Bay.

The Cornell Manual for
Lifeboatmen, Able Seamen, and
Qualified Members of Engine Department

1. The Lifeboatman

Disaster may strike suddenly and take many forms. Fires, collisions, explosions, and sinkings are not announced ahead of time, but they take their toll in death and injuries. For this reason, every American ship has a station bill giving the alarm signals and setting forth the emergency duties for each member of the crew.

Station Bills and Muster Lists

When you join a ship, learn your job immediately, and in the event of emergency, know your responsibilities as set forth in the station bill. You must also know the alarm signals. (A numbered card should be fixed on each berth or issued to each crew member at the time of reporting aboard so that you will know your individual duties in case of danger.)

The lifeboatman in charge of each lifeboat or life raft must have a muster list giving the name and abandon ship duties of each member of his lifeboat crew. These duties, set forth in the station bill and muster list, include assembling and guiding the passengers and assisting them with the adjustment of their life preservers. The usual procedure is to have the muster list for each boat typed and then laminated or placed in plastic to protect it from the weather.

A sample station bill giving the standard emergency signals and examples of how duties should be assigned follows. The master may prescribe other signals in the station bill that he deems necessary, such as signals for assembling the emergency squad. The individual duties would be those

MATSON NAVIGATION COMPANY

STATION BILL

S.S. ____

SIGNALS

FIRE OR EMERGENCY—Continuous Sounding of Ship's Whistle and Continuous Ringing of GENERAL ALARM Bell for at least 10 Seconds, Preceded and/or Followed by Location Signal:

1 Short Ring on General Alarm Bell	**FIRE FORWARD**
2 Short Rings on General Alarm Bell	**FIRE AMIDSHIPS**
4 Short Rings on General Alarm Bell	**FIRE AFT**

ABANDON SHIP—7 Short Blasts followed by 1 Long Blast on Ship's Whistle accompanied by the Same Signal on the General Alarm Bell
MAN OVERBOARD—5 Short Blasts on Ship's Whistle and 5 Short Rings on General Alarm Bell
DISMISS FROM ANY DRILL—3 Short Blasts on Ship's Whistle and 3 Short Rings on General Alarm Bell

LOWER BOATS	1 Short Whistle Blast
STOP LOWERING BOATS	2 Short Whistle Blasts

INSTRUCTIONS

1. Immediately upon Reporting Aboard for Duty Ascertain Your Emergency Stations and Duties. Become Familiar with the Layout of the Vessel and the Quickest Means of Proceeding to Your Station from Your Normal Place of Work or Quarters.
2. All Drills on this Vessel Will Simulate Actual Emergency Conditions. Order Must be Maintained at All Drills.
3. Upon Hearing Emergency Signal Proceed Quickly and Safely to Your Emergency Station.
4. EMERGENCY SQUAD Assemble with Designated Equipment at Scene of Fire under Direction of Chief Officer. Emergency Equipment on this Vessel is Stowed SECOND DECK, OUTSIDE CO-2 ROOM
5. Men Manning Deck Fire Stations, not in Fire Area, Stand by Hydrant and Await Orders of Officer in Charge.
6. Men on Watch Remain on Watch Until Relieved.
7. IN CASE OF FIRE—Sound Alarm at Once—Stop All Blowers—Close All Kingpost Dampers and Trim All Cowl Ventilators Off the Wind—Start Fire Pumps—Close All Airports and Weather Doors—ISOLATE—EXTINGUISH—COOL.
8. FOR MAN OVERBOARD—Hail and Pass the Word "MAN OVERBOARD" to the Bridge, Throw Illuminated Ring Buoys Over, Post Lookout Aloft, Stop Engines (if conditions warrant), Deck Department and Emergency Squad Muster at Lee Lifeboat.
9. Wear Your Lifejacket to All Abandon Ship Drills. Lifejacket Must Be Worn, or Carried, to All Other Drills.
10. Crew Members are Interdependent, one upon the other, in Any Emergency. Learn to Perform Your Emergency Duties in a Competent Manner. Familiarity with the Proper Use of Emergency Equipment May Save a Life. It Could Be YOURS! All Crew Members will Assist as Required by the Officer in Charge Until the Signal for Dismissal is Sounded.
11. Steward's Department to Arouse, Warn and Direct Passengers to Lifeboat Stations—Seeing They are Warmly Dressed and Lifejackets Properly Adjusted.

RATING	CARD No.	FIRE AND EMERGENCY DUTIES	CARD BOAT No.	No.	ABANDON SHIP DUTIES
DECK DEPARTMENT					
MASTER	-A-	IN COMMAND	-A-	1	IN COMMAND
CHIEF OFFICER	2	MUSTER EMERGENCY SQUAD, IN CHARGE AT SCENE OF FIRE.	1	2	IN COMMAND, IN CHARGE LOWERING ALL BOATS.
SECOND OFFICER	2	IN CHARGE FORWARD DECK, BOW TO AFT END ROW #1, FRAME 155.	2	1	SECOND IN COMMAND, MUSTER CREW, CLEAR & LOWER BOAT.

Rating	No.	Duty
ABLE SEAMAN	20	"K DECK TO SECURE GRIPE.
ABLE SEAMAN	21	" TO SECURE GRIPE.
		"" GRIPE.

ENGINE DEPARTMENT

	20	
	21	

Rating	No.	No.	Duty
CHIEF ENGINEER	101	1	IN CHARGE PROPELLING MACHINERY.
FIRST ASSISTANT	102	2	IN CHARGE OF ENGINE ROOM.
SECOND ASSISTANT	103	1	IN CHARGE CONTROLS, CO-2 SMOTHERING SYSTEM. STOP ALL PUMPS WITH OVERBOARD DISCHARGE ABOVE WATERLINE.
THIRD ASSISTANT	104		FORWARD MACHINERY ROOM – IN CHARGE FIRE PUMPS. OPERATE MOTOR IN LIFEBOAT
THIRD ASSISTANT	105	116	ENGINE ROOM – IN CHARGE FIRE PUMPS. ……ER LIFERAFT – IN CHARGE LAUNCHING AFTER LIFERAFT #2.
THIRD ASSISTANT	106	117	ENGINE ROOM – ASSIST CHIEF E… "" ASSIST WITH LAUNCHING AFTER LIFERAFT #2.
CHIEF ELECTRICIAN	107	118	ENGINE ROOM – ASSIST C… "ST WITH LAUNCHING AFTER LIFERAFT #2.
SECOND ELECTRICIAN	108	119	EMERGENCY GENERA… " FAST AFTER FRAPPING LINE.
REEFER MAINTENANCE	109	120	EMERGENCY G… " AFTER FRAPPING LINE.
UNLICENSED JR. ENGINEER	110	121	REEFER "SSIBLE. ATTEND CRANK WHEN HOISTING.
UNLICENSED JR. ENGINEER	11'	122	EN… ", ATTEND CRANK WHEN HOISTING.
UNLICENSED JR. ENGIN…			"N CRANK WHEN HOISTING.
WIPER			
WIPER			

STEWARD'S DEPARTMENT

Rating	No.	No.	Duty
CHIEF STEWARD	201	201	1	CLOSE WEATHER DOORS AFTER HOUSE, STANDBY HOSPITAL. LEAD OUT SEA PAINTER AS FAR AS POSSIBLE.
CHIEF COOK	202	209	SECURE GALLEY RANGES, ATTEND STRETCHER. "AD OUT SEA PAINTER AS FAR AS POSSIBLE.
SECOND COOK & BAKER	203	210	CLOSE WATERTIGHT DOORS, 2ND D… PAINTER FROM BOAT DECK, ATTEND CRANK WHEN HOISTING.
ASSISTANT COOK/MESSMAN	204	211	CLOSE WATERTIGHT DOORS. ' . FROM BOAT DECK, ATTEND CRANK WHEN HOISTING.
SALOON WAITER	205	212	FIRE HYDRANTS #19 ' "DER, ATTEND CRANK WHEN HOISTING, PROVIDE BLANKETS.
CREW MESSMAN	206		FIRE HYDRANTS …ATION OF FIRE STATIONS ATTEND CRANK WHEN HOISTING, PROVIDE BLANKETS.
OFFICERS B.R.	207		CLOSE WEA…CASTLE HEAD, ABREAST ANCHOR WINDLASS "D CRANK WHEN HOISTING, PROVIDE BLANKETS.
STEWARD UTILITY	208	301	FIRE : . – UPPER DECK, ON HATCH COAMING ROW #3 "K WHEN HOISTING, PROVIDE BLANKETS.
	209	302	FIRE . – UPPER DECK, PORT SIDE, ON HATCH COAMING ROW #12
	'..	303	#20 – UPPER DECK, STBD SIDE, ON HATCH COAMING ROW #14
	303		#37 – UPPER DECK, STERN, NEAR SPARES HATCH
			#33 & #34 – UPPER DECK, ABREAST GANGWAY.

NOTES: 1. Any rating not carried on a vessel is to be marked "Not Carried" or stricken out.
2. Additional ratings are to be inserted in appropriate blank spaces provided for the purpose.
3. For additional information see NOTICE entitled STATION BILLS AND REPORTS OF MASTERS, FORM CG 809A (or B)

MASTER

Fig. 1. The station bill for S.S. *Maui*, 26,665-deadweight-ton containership owned by Matson Navigation Company. Courtesy Matson Navigation Company.

considered appropriate by each shipmaster to meet the needs of his own vessel.

Lifeboatman Certification and Requirements

Certification required. Every person employed in a rating as lifeboatman on any U.S. vessel requiring certificated lifeboatmen shall produce a certificate as lifeboatman or merchant mariner's document endorsed as lifeboatman or able seaman before signing articles of agreement. No certificate of efficiency as lifeboatman is required of any person employed on any unrigged vessel, except on a seagoing barge and on a tank barge navigating waters other than rivers and/or canals.

Service or training requirements. An applicant, to be eligible for certification as lifeboatman, must meet one of the following requirements:

1. At least 1 year's sea service in the deck department, or at least 2 years' sea service in the other departments of ocean, coastwise, Great Lakes, and other lakes, bays, or sounds vessels;
2. Graduation from a schoolship approved by and conducted under rules prescribed by the Commandant;
3. Satisfactory completion of basic training by a Cadet of the U.S. Merchant Marine Cadet Corps;
4. Satisfactory completion of 3 years' training at the U.S. Naval Academy or the U.S. Coast Guard Academy, including two training cruises;
5. Satisfactory completion of a course of training approved by the Commandant and served aboard a training vessel;
6. Successful completion of a training course approved by the Commandant, such course to include a minimum of 30 hours' actual lifeboat training: *Provided,* that the applicant produces evidence of having served a minimum of 3 months at sea aboard ocean or coastwise vessels.

An applicant, to be eligible for certification as lifeboatman, shall be able to speak and understand the English language as would be required in the rating of lifeboatman and in an emergency aboard ship.

Examination and demonstration of ability. Before a lifeboatman's certificate may be granted, the applicant must prove to the satisfaction of the Coast Guard by oral or written examination and by actual demonstration that:

1. He has been trained in all the operations connected with the launching of lifeboats and life rafts and the use of oars and sails;
2. He is acquainted with the practical handling of boats themselves; and,
3. He is capable of taking command of a boat's crew.

The oral or written examination is conducted in the English language and consists of seventy multiple-choice questions administered by the Coast Guard regarding:

1. Lifeboats and life rafts, the names of their essential parts, and a description of the required equipment;
2. The clearing away, swinging out, and lowering of lifeboats and life rafts; the handling of lifeboats under oars and sails, including questions relative to the proper handling of a boat in a heavy sea; and,
3. The operation and functions of commonly used types of davits.

The practical examination is a demonstration of ability which is normally conducted by the vessel master, but which may be witnessed by the Coast Guard Examining Officer, Coast Guard Marine Inspector, or a responsible person authorized in writing by the Officer in Charge, Marine Inspection. He will sign a letter stating that the candidate has demonstrated his ability in operations connected with the launching of lifeboats and life rafts including the carrying out of the usual orders given, in the practical handling of lifeboats, and in taking command of a lifeboat crew. The candidate may then present this letter to a Coast Guard Marine Inspection or Safety Office as evidence of satisfactory completion of all requirements and may be issued a merchant mariner's document endorsed for lifeboatman.

General provisions respecting merchant mariner's documents endorsed as lifeboatman. A merchant mariner's document endorsed as able seaman shall be considered as the equivalent of a certificate as lifeboatman or an endorsement as lifeboatman and it shall be accepted as a certificate as lifeboatman wherever required by law or regulation.

Lifeboats

The following pages describe the lifesaving gear found on merchant vessels and set forth the methods for handling such equipment.

All lifeboats must have the ship's name and the number of the boat marked or painted on each bow in figures not less than 3 inches high. Also the top of thwarts, side benches, and footings of lifeboats shall be painted or otherwise colored international orange. The area in way of the red mechanical disengaging gear control lever, from the keel to the side bench, shall be painted or otherwise colored white, to provide a contrasting background for the lever. This band of white should be approximately 12 inches wide, depending on the internal arrangement of the lifeboat. The oars shall be conspicuously marked with the vessel's name. When there are lifeboats on both sides of the ship, odd numbers are given the starboard boats and even numbers are given the port boats. Lifeboat No. 1 will be the forward boat on the starboard side; lifeboat No. 2 will be the forward boat on the port side; lifeboat No. 3 will be next abaft lifeboat No. 1 on the starboard side; lifeboat No. 4 next abaft lifeboat No. 2 on the port side, etc. Under wartime or national emergency conditions the nesting of lifeboats can be authorized. In this event, the lifeboat under lifeboat No. 1 is numbered 1-A; the lifeboat under lifeboat No. 2 is numbered 2-A, etc. Nesting of lifeboats is not permitted under peacetime conditions.

The cubical contents and the number of persons allowed to be carried are also marked or painted on each lifeboat in letters or numbers not less than 1½ inches high. In addition,

Fig. 2. Open lifeboat in gravity davits. Boat is secured for sea. Sea painter is rigged. Tricing pendant is clearly shown. Note that one end is secured to a padeye on the davit arm and the other to the MacCluney hook. A lifeboat may be constructed of galvanized steel, aluminum, or fiberglass.

the number of persons allowed shall be marked or painted on top of at least two thwarts in letters and numbers not less than 3 inches high. A builder's plate on the bow plating gives this and other information.

Lifeboats are normally pointed at both ends, this design having been found most seaworthy. They are provided with air tanks or buoyancy materials so that the boat will float even though full of water, with all gear, and a capacity load of persons aboard. The air tanks are placed along the sides so that the boat resists being turned over or capsized under flooded conditions. A great deal of care has gone into the design and construction of lifeboats and *no changes should be made without the approval of the Coast Guard.* Only in an emergency may repairs be made without Coast Guard approval. Such repairs must be reported as soon as practicable to the Officer in Charge, Marine Inspection, in the first port of call after the repairs are made.

Lifeboats differ in their construction, but certain features are common to all. These features should be known because they are important in the handling and maintenance of these craft.

A *keel* on a metal boat is made of a heavy rectangular metal bar carefully joined to the *stem* and *stern posts* to form the backbone of the boat. The *garboard strake* of plating is fitted next to the keel by riveting or, in some cases, welding. The stem and stern posts each have a hole near the top for a shackle pin. The stern post is provided with *gudgeons* for holding the rudder. A *gunwale* running the length of the boat between the stem and stern posts is fitted atop the lifeboat's plating on each side. The gunwales are sturdy and help the keel give lengthwise strength to the boat. To the gunwales are fitted sockets for the rowlocks and brackets to help support the thwarts. The top rows of plating just below the gunwales are known as the *sheer* strakes.

Near the turn of the *bilges, grab rails* are provided on the outside of the boat for persons to cling to should it overturn in the water. The grab rail is secured to small plates by fewer rivets than the number of rivets used to secure these plates in turn to the hull of the boat. If the grab rail should be torn off, the possibility of causing holes in the shell plating is reduced by this method of attachment. Where there are no grab rails, knotted lines of 2-inch Manila rope passed from gunwale to gunwale under the keel can serve as *grab lines* for the same purpose.

Where the lifeboat fits in the chocks, cradles, or against puddings, *doubler plating* is used. The doublers give added strength but are subject to wear and corrosion where the boat works in the chocks or against the puddings and should be examined when the boat is lifted or swung out. These areas require painting more frequently than other parts of a lifeboat's plating.

Aluminum lifeboats may be damaged by electrolytic corrosion if steel or some other metals are allowed in contact. Electrolysis may occur in a salt air atmosphere even if the dissimilar metals do not actually touch. No steel or iron tools should be left in aluminum boats.

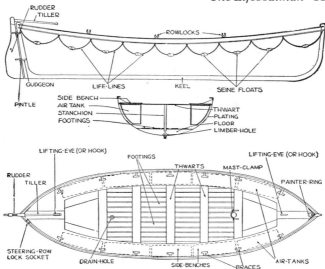

Fig. 3. A metallic open lifeboat. This boat is fitted with rowlocks for oars. More frequently hand-propelling equipment (Fleming gear) is used. A lifeboat with a capacity of 100 or more must be motorized. The more modern enclosed lifeboat is shown in figure. 4.

One or more drains are provided in each lifeboat to allow water to run out when the boat is out of the water. A small metal cage forms part of the drain extending below the shell of the boat. Within the cage, a rubber ball floats when the boat is in the water to act as an automatic closing valve. If there is rubbish in the cage, the ball cannot do its job. A cap is secured to each drain by a short length of small chain so it is ready for closing off the drain before the boat is launched. Drains should be kept clean at all times, the rubber ball should be in good condition, and *the drain cap should be screwed on before the boat is launched.*

On the bottom of the boat, or on the *floors* of larger boats, are placed the *bottom boards* or *footings.* These spread out the weight of persons or equipment over a wide area of the thin plating and contribute slightly to the strength of the boat. Footings are secured in a manner that allows them to

Fig. 4. One of the comparatively recent developments in lifesaving equipment is the enclosed lifeboat, shown here on Miranda gravity davits aboard *Chevron Mississippi*. It is constructed of fire retardant fiberglass and painted international orange. Sufficient buoyance is provided to make the boat unsinkable under all conditions up to a full load. A marine diesel fitted with a hydraulic gearbox can propel the boat at approximately 6½ knots. Boats of this type may be equipped with complete life-support systems to allow operation in water covered with burning oil. Courtesy Watercraft America and W.B. Arnold Co., Inc.

be removed for painting or other maintenance work on the bottom of the boat.

The *thwarts* or seats extend from side to side in the boat. When the depth of the boat below the thwarts is *too* far for a rower's legs to reach the footings, foot rests or *stretchers* are provided. The thwarts are not only important as seats, they help to provide the athwartship strength of the boat in the same manner as the beams of a ship. Additional seating capacity is given by the *side benches*. Brackets from the gunwales help to stiffen and support the thwarts and side benches. If the boat is wide, upright stanchions are placed beneath the thwarts to help support the weight. The extreme forward seating is called the *bow sheets*, and the extreme after seating is called the *stern sheets*.

Provision tanks and *air tanks* for buoyancy are placed beneath the side benches and thwarts. Generally, such tanks

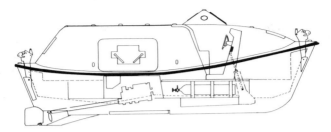

Fig. 5. Cutaway side view of enclosed lifeboat. Courtesy Watercraft America and W.B. Arnold Co., Inc.

are made so that they can be removed for painting and other maintenance work. Each tank is fitted with a small nipple so that its airtightness can be checked without removing it from the stowed position. This can be done with a small air pump. Even a pump is unnecessary, as a man using a short length of rubber tubing can blow enough air through the nipple to cause the flat sides of most tanks to bulge if the tank is airtight. For very small leaks, the cap must be replaced when pressure is inside, as it would require some time for the leakage to be noticeable.

Seamen often can tell whether a tank is tight by observing it on a hot day. If the flat sides of any tank are not bulged like its neighboring tanks, there is a likelihood that it is leaking. When a tank holds air pressure, escaping air can be felt when the cap on the nipple is removed. Leaks can be located by brushing soapy water over the tank when there is air pressure inside. Bubbles will appear where the air is leaking out of the tank. Another method is to hold the tank under water so that escaping bubbles will reveal the leaks. *When tanks are removed for any purpose, they should be restowed in the original position.*

Unicellular plastic foam, polystyrene (Styrofoam), can be authorized to fill air tanks. This material, which consists of a plastic with a large number of small air cavities, will not absorb water, and will permit an air tank to be used which is no longer airtight.

A *mast hasp* and *step* are installed on each boat supplied with a sail. The step receives the bottom of the mast. The *hasp* is attached to a thwart and, assisted by the *wire stays*, holds the mast erect.

Many lifeboats are constructed with diesel engines. To avoid injuring people during drills, the deck area about the propeller should be kept clear. Motorboats have overboard openings in the shell for cooling water to enter, a clutch to permit idling the engine, and a reversing gear. Where the propeller shaft passes out of the *stern tube*, a *stern gland* prevents water from entering the boat. Fuel tanks for power-driven boats are built to keep danger from fire or explosion to a minimum, but care is necessary to keep open flames away from fuel or vapor that may be present. Motorboat engines must be operated each time abandon-ship drills are held, but unless the boat is put in the water, the lack of cooling water through the engine limits the time the engine can be run without overheating.

Hand-propelling gear is installed on some lifeboats. This type of propulsion has a propeller, stern tube, stern gland, and gears but, instead of using an engine, power is furnished by pushing and pulling lever handles fore and aft. The bottom ends of the lever handles fit into sockets connected to a bar on each side of the boat. These two bars move cranks on the sides of the gear box near the boat's stern. Gear boxes, on engine-driven as well as hand-propelled boats, *must be kept free of water.* In cold weather this water can freeze and make it impossible for the gears to rotate and propel the boat. *The bars, cranks, and levers for hand-propelled boats must be kept clear when stowing gear.*

Whatever the means may be for propelling a lifeboat, as many of the crew as possible ought to be familiar with the method of operation. For motor-driven boats, the process of starting and stopping the engine, operating the clutch, reverse gear, and speed control should be known by all seamen who could be called on to operate the boat in an emergency.

A *rudder* is provided each boat for steering. The rudder is turned by means of a *tiller*, which fits on the upper part of the rudder called the *rudder stock*. A toggle pin attached to

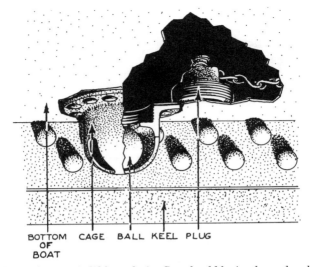

BOTTOM CAGE BALL KEEL PLUG
OF
BOAT

Fig. 6. Automatic lifeboat drain. Cap should be in place when boat is launched, although rubber ball will float and act as a check valve to keep water from entering boat. Drain must be kept clean and free from debris.

the rudder or tiller by a small chain is used to secure the tiller in place. The rudder has *pintles*, metal pieces which fit into the *gudgeons* on the stern post. To simplify rigging the rudder in the water, the lower pintle is made so it can be slipped into its gudgeon before the upper pintle is engaged. Upper gudgeons are usually of a sliding latch type, into which the pintle, in the form of an eyebolt, can be placed. Rudders are made of wood for most boats. When metal is used, it is formed into a watertight hollow casing, so that it will float. A test nipple allows testing the watertightness. Because the size of a lifeboat rudder is larger in proportion to the size of the boat than the rudder of a large ship, lifeboats are relatively easy to maneuver. In addition to a rudder, a large oar known as the *steering oar* is required for each boat.

Releasing gear is installed in lifeboats to let go the falls. Without such gear, letting go the falls in a seaway could be a difficult and dangerous job. The widely used Rottmer gear releases the falls at both ends of the boat at the same time. The man in charge of the boat turns a lever. This lever rotates shafting connected through universal joints to hook locks at both bow and stern ends of the boat. When the hook locks are opened, the hooks release the falls even though there may be weight on them.

While releasing gear helps to launch a boat safely in a seaway, its careless or unintentional use has led to serious accidents. Regulations require that the lever be painted red and marked: Danger—Lever Drops Boat. The person in charge of a boat must be sure that his crew knows that turning the lever at the wrong time can drop the boat from a height and seriously injure those in the boat. Regulations also provide that the top of thwarts, side benches, and footings of lifeboats shall be painted or otherwise colored international orange. The area in way of the red mechanical disengaging gear control lever, from the keel to the side bench, shall be painted or otherwise colored white, to provide a contrasting background for the lever. This band of white should be approximately 12 inches wide, depending on the internal arrangement of the lifeboat. When men are painting or working in boats hung on the davits, a wise precaution is to secure the boat independently of the falls with several turns of wire rope from the stem and stern post shackles to the davits.

Whenever the boat is in the water, it is good to work the releasing gear several times to see that it moves freely. At this time, note whether both hook locks open at the same time, as release of the bow fall before the stern fall with a ship underway could have serious consequences.

Rottmer-type releasing gear hooks are fitted with preventer bars (see figure 7). These bars prevent the falls from accidentally becoming detached when the boat is waterborne, when there is no weight on the falls.

Because the task of getting a boat and its complement safely in and out of the water is the most hazardous part of lifeboat handling, considerable attention has been given to the releasing gear. It is a helpful device in competent hands,

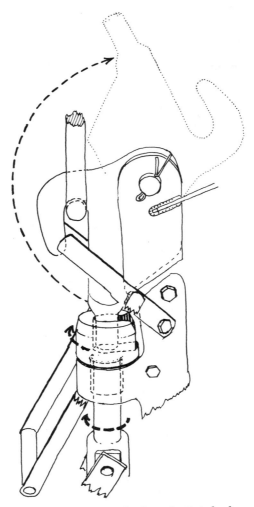

Fig. 7. Rottmer releasing gear. As the red-painted release lever is tripped on orders of the boat commander, the universal joint rotates. This forces the hook to move in the "up" position, and the boat is freed from the falls. Prior to recovery the release lever must be rotated back to its normal position so that the boat can once again be "hooked" onto the falls.

but if it is entrusted to an untrained individual, it could be misused and cause a serious accident.

Equipment for lifeboats. Lifeboats are provided with equipment to assure that necessary items for survival and alerting rescuers are available. The names of these items, a brief description, and the methods for their use follow:

Bailer—A simple device similar to a dustpan but often made of wood or fiberglass for scooping water out of the boat.

Bilge pump—A pump fitted with hose, strainer, and foot valve and operated by a back and forth, or rotary motion of the operation lever. These pumps are designed to rid the boat of water with less effort than by bailing.

Boat hooks—Wooden poles tipped with a metal ball-point and hook. These poles are used for fending off, hooking falls when coming alongside, etc. One should be available for the bow and one for the stern of each boat.

Buckets—Two buckets of galvanized iron or other corrosion resistant metal are required. Each should have a 6-foot lanyard of 12-thread line. In addition to their obvious uses, buckets can be used as emergency sea anchors. A frequent misuse of buckets is for stowage of lanterns or similar equipment. Water may accumulate in an upright bucket left lashed under a thwart, with resulting damage to equipment left in it.

Compass and mounting—A small magnetic compass is provided in each lifeboat. Unless a man familiar with the correction for variation and deviation is one of the boat's crew, simple directions given on the container should be carefully read before the compass is used. These instructions are as follows:

> To find compass error using the sun, moon, star, or cloud while near the horizon, suppose: The sun is rising and the compass is mounted in place. Head boat west by compass and you decide the sun is bearing 70° by the compass. Head boat east by compass and suppose the sun bears 100°. These added together make 170°, and when halved make 85°, which is the correct bearing of the sun at that moment.

Now suppose you want to steer southwest. Head the boat 225° by compass and take another bearing of the sun. It now bears 65°; it should bear 85°. Therefore, the compass card is turned 20° too far to the right giving a 20° error; thus you should steer 20° to the left to offset it or 205° by compass to make good 225°, the direction you want. If it is desired to remove this error, proceed as outlined in manufacturer's instructions.

Ditty bag—A canvas bag containing a sailmaker's palm, needles, sail twine, marline, and a marlinespike.

Drinking cups—These should have a 3-foot lanyard of ⅛ inch cotton line.

Fire extinguishers—These are attached at each end of motor-propelled boats.

First aid kit—Instructions for use of the contents of the first aid kit are attached to the inside of the cover. The contents include bandages, eye dressing with ointment, tourniquet, forceps, scissors, safety pins, wire splint, ammonia inhalants, iodine applicators, aspirin and acetaminophen (Tylenol), and petrolatum gauze.

Flashlight—Three spare cells (or one 3 cell spare), and 2 spare bulbs are required for the flashlight. Batteries must be replaced yearly during the annual stripping, cleaning, and overhaul of the lifeboat. Flashlights approved for use in lifeboats are so designed that they can be used for blinker signaling.

Hatchets—These are secured by lanyards at each end of the boat so as to be handy for cutting falls or painters if this becomes necessary.

Heaving line—A buoyant 1-inch line 10 fathoms long.

Jackknife—One blade is a can opener for opening food and water tins.

Lantern—Containing enough oil to burn for 9 hours; must be kept ready for immediate use.

Lifeboat gunwale ladder—Required only on boats with a capacity of 60 or more persons, must be secured about midships on the boat in such a way as to be ready for immediate use.

Lifeline—Made of at least 12-thread line in bights of 3 feet or less, with a seine float in each bight, must hang within 12 inches of the water when the lifeboat is light. The lifeline is provided for swimmers to hang onto or for use of people who are unable to find space in a crowded boat. Buoyant lifelines do not require seine floats.

Life preservers—Two are provided in each boat in addition to those provided on board ship for each crew member.

Locker—A suitable stowage space for small items of equipment which will protect them from the elements.

Mast and sail—A standing lug rig with spars and equipment is provided on all oar-propelled lifeboats. The sail is colored international orange so that it stands out against the sea. There must be a cover to protect the sail from the weather. Sails should be aired often to avoid mildew.

Matches—These must be kept dry. A watertight can stowed in the equipment locker or under the stern thwart can be used. Dipping the can in hot paraffin wax helps to keep the matches in good condition.

Milk, condensed—One pound for each person of the lifeboat's authorized complement should be stowed in the boat's lockers.

Mirrors, signaling—These simple devices have proved to be effective in showing the location of a lifeboat to rescue ships or planes. There are several types, each having instructions on its package setting forth the proper method for its use. The instructions for the use of the rear-sight-type signaling mirror follow:

1. Observer should face a point between the sun and ship or plane to which he wants to signal.
2. Hold the mirror in one hand about 4 inches from the face and sight the ship or plane to be signaled through the hole in the mirror.
3. Hold the other hand about 12 inches behind the mirror in line with the sun and the hole through the mirror, so that a small spot of light appears on the hand. The small spot of light on the hand is reflected on the back face of the mirror (side toward the observer).

4. Now tilt the mirror so that the spot of light on the back face of the mirror disappears through the hole in the mirror, at the same time keeping the ship or plane in sight through the hole. With the mirror in this position, the light rays from the sun will be reflected to the ship or plane.

   Note: When the angle between the sun and the ship or plane is small, the spot of light will appear on the face

Fig. 8. Sighting a rear-sight-type signaling mirror.

of the observer, thus allowing both hands to be used in tilting the mirror.

Oars—Pulling boats are equipped with the proper number of rowing oars and a steering oar. Figure 9 gives the name for the parts of an oar. The name of the ship must be marked on all oars.

Oil, illuminating—In addition to the oil carried in the lantern, an additional quart is required for refilling if this becomes necessary.

Oil, storm—One gallon of vegetable, fish, or animal oil must be carried in the metal container fitted at the apex of the sea anchor so that it can be easily distributed on the water to reduce the drag of the wind on the water, thus helping to prevent breaking seas. Mineral oil, such as fuel or lube oil, is not used because it is less effective.

Painter—Lifeboats in deep-sea service need a sea painter and a boat painter, each of at least 2¾-inch circumference Manila rope. The painter must be at least 3 times as long as the distance between the boat deck and the waterline when the ship is light. The boat painter is made fast to the stem by a shackle through a spliced eye and is used to hold the boat alongside. The sea painter has a long spliced eye which can be bent around a thwart and secured with a toggle. It is used when the ship is underway or there is a current to veer the boat away from alongside. It should be made fast to the side of the thwart nearest the ship. The toggle, made of hardwood, should have a lanyard made of small stuff. The end of the lanyard is secured to the thwart, not the painter, so that the toggle cannot injure anyone when the sea painter is released. This will also keep the toggle available in the boat where it is needed.

Fig. 9. Parts of an oar.

Fig. 10. A sea painter.

Plugs—These are the closures provided for the automatic drains. They should be attached to the lifeboat by a small chain in a handy position for use. Some patented drains have a screw-down cover.

Provisions—Two pounds of provisions for each person of the boat's authorized complement are carried in the lockers.

Rowlocks—Each oar is provided with a rowlock which is attached to the boat by a small chain near its proper place. Two spare rowlocks are also carried in the equipment locker.

Rudder and tiller—Since the rudder and tiller must be shipped before or soon after the boat is launched, they should be kept available in the stern of the boat.

Sea anchor—This device is used to hold the boat end onto (or into) wind and sea. The trip line permits the sea anchor to be easily brought back aboard the lifeboat. Since the trip line provided with the sea anchor is only 15 feet long, it is necessary to lengthen it with the heaving line or other line available (see figure 11).

Floating orange smoke distress signals—This daytime signal alerts planes and ships to the presence of the boat. It is ignited by means of a pull wire and then thrown overboard to leeward. These signals are only approved for use up to 3 years after the date of manufacture.

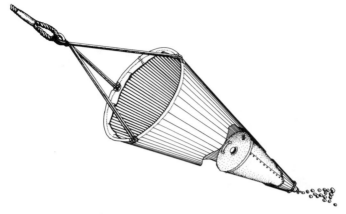

Fig. 11. A lifeboat sea anchor.

Red hand distress flares—Twelve hand-held flares are carried. Each is ignited by removing the cap on the end and scratching the button on the flare against the scratch surface on the cap. These signals are only approved for use up to 3 years after the date of manufacture.

Red parachute distress flares—Twelve cartridges and a pistol or 12 hand-held rocket-propelled flares are carried. These red flares reach several hundred feet above the water and can be seen at night for considerable distances. Flares are only approved for use up to 3 years after the date of manufacture.

Water—Nine sealed cans containing 3 quarts for each person of the lifeboat's authorized complement are carried in the lockers. These cans must be replaced at least every 5 years.

Radio installation—Required only for motor-propelled lifeboats with a radio cabin.

Tool kit—Required for motor-propelled lifeboats. Contains the following tools: 1 12-ounce ball peen hammer, 1 screwdriver with 6-inch blade, 1 pair 8-inch slip joint pliers, and 1 8-inch adjustable end wrench.

The equipment listed is that for the lifeboats of ocean or coastwise vessels. Great Lakes and Inland craft carry items appropriate for such service. Rafts carry similar but lesser amounts of equipment.

Lifeboats, rafts, etc., may carry equipment in addition to the required amounts only if it does not interfere with seating or seaworthiness of the boat and does not overload the davit.

Check-off lists can be used to assure that all the equipment required is in the boat. The information necessary to compile such a list is available in the Rules and Regulations which apply to the type of ship and route upon which she is sailing. Booklets providing this information can be obtained free of charge at Coast Guard Marine Inspection Offices.

Davits, Winches, Blocks, and Falls

Although there may be a few exceptions which allow the use of other gear, in all normal circumstances davits are required aboard merchant vessels for the lowering and hoisting of lifeboats. Davits are installed in pairs and can be extended over the water from the side of the ship in order to lower or hoist the lifeboat by means of wire rope or fiber falls, which are attached to the heads of the davit arms.

There are three general types of davits: radial or round bar, mechanical, and gravity. A further development of the gravity davit is the Miranda gravity davit, especially designed for use with enclosed lifeboats.

Although the older radial and mechanical davits are rarely found on modern merchant ships, a description of them must be given:

Radial davits. In moving the boat from the inboard to the outboard position, the heads of the davit arms swing in horizontal arcs and do not raise or lower as do the heads of the other davit types. The boat is swung aft until the bow clears the forward davit arm; then the boat is swung outboard and forward to the lowering position. Hand turning-out gears may be attached to each davit arm to insure that the boat can be swung outboard when the ship is listing

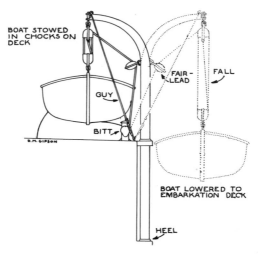

Fig. 12. A radial or round bar davit. Radial davits have not been installed in new construction ships in the American merchant marine for many years. They require a considerable number of men to launch or recover a lifeboat. They may still be seen occasionally on smaller vessels or yachts.

heavily. Though radial davits are easily designed and manufactured, the difficulty of swinging out a heavy boat with these davits prevents their use on large ships. Only small vessels are allowed to carry radial davits.

Mechanical davits. The two common mechanical davits are the sheath screw and the quadrantal davits. These two types may be further described by terms which refer to the shape of the davit arm, either straight boom or crescent. For all types, the davit arm is cranked out by screws, gears, or other mechanical means, and it moves outboard in a plane which is perpendicular to the side of the ship.

Gravity davits. Gravity davits have been required on all new construction merchant ships for a number of years. Although there are several types, all of them depend upon gravity to launch the boat. Power is not used except when raising the boat. After the release of the locking bars, these davits move from the inboard to the outboard position with

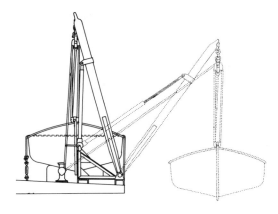

Fig. 13. A sheath screw boom davit. Sheath screw and quadrantal davits (shown in fig. 15(A)), are also called mechanical davits, and are an improvement on the original radial davit. The sheath screw boom and sheath screw crescent davit (fig. 14) operate in exactly the same way. They were installed in World War II Liberty ships. Launching procedure is far easier than on the radial davit. They are not, however, approved for new construction.

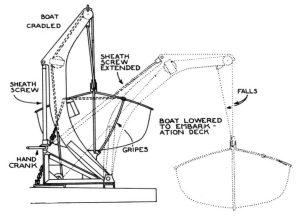

Fig. 14. A sheath screw crescent davit.

no application of force except that which is needed to lift the winch brake handle. The most common gravity davit consists of two davit arms which ride on rollers down fixed trackways to the outboard position. Another type is pivoted at the lower ends of both davit arms, which move outboard through a system of mechanical linkages. One man, who must remain aboard ship, can lower a lifeboat from the secured position to the water. Gravity davits are required for larger lifeboats. The most recent developments are the Miranda gravity davit and the pivot gravity davit, which are especially designed for the use of enclosed lifeboats. Both are common on tankers. These davits are illustrated in figure 16(A) and 16(B). On both installations, the lifeboat commander can lower the boat from the embarkation deck to the water from his position in the boat itself. Both davit installations and launching procedures vary dependent upon the time period when the davits were installed, as well as any modifications that may have been necessary to fit them to their parent ship. Consequently, it is extremely important to be completely familiar with the launching procedures posted by the davits as well as by the coxswain's console in the lifeboat. The prudent seaman will never be dependent on someone else to teach him something in an emergency which he should have learned ahead of time.

Boat falls. With radial davits, fiber rope falls are used, but on gravity davits, wire is always employed. Mechanical davits use either wire or rope.

Fiber rope falls are rove through blocks at the ends of the davits and at the ends of the boat for the mechanical advantage and increased strength afforded by multiple parts. The boats are lowered by paying out the rope over cruciform bitts or cleats provided for the purpose.

Fiber rope is stowed on reels or coiled in boxes. These should be covered to keep off ice and snow, and to protect the rope from exposure to the weather. Good operating practice with Manila or synthetic fall is to "end for end" them after one year, i.e., reverse the lead of the falls to insure more even wear, and to renew them after two years. The replaced rope

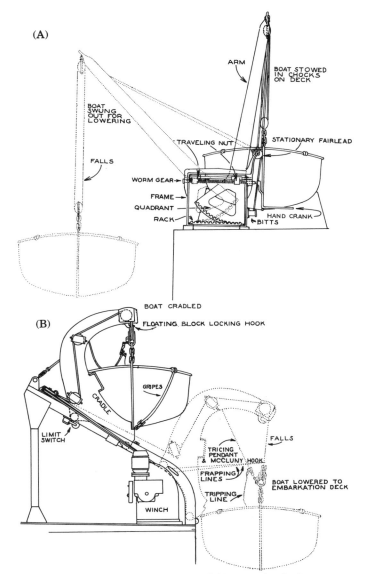

Fig. 15. (A) a quadrantal davit and (B) a gravity davit.

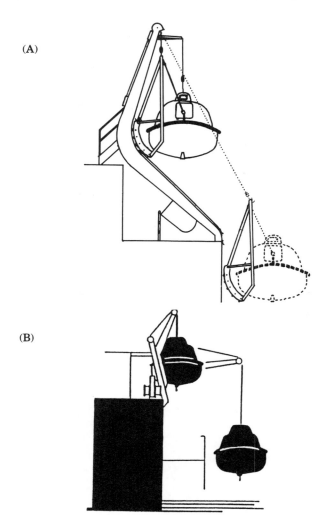

(A)

(B)

Fig. 16. (A) A Miranda gravity davit. Miranda davits are designed for use with enclosed lifeboats. Figure 4 shows the installation of a Miranda davit. (B) The pivot gravity davit, which has one pivot point for each arm. The falls are led between the davits via a crossbeam, leaving the deck clear of wire. The boat is stowed in such a way as to leave the deck beneath clear. Courtesy W.B. Arnold Co., Inc.

can be used for less critical purposes than lifesaving equipment.

Wire rope falls are handled from a winch. An automatic brake limits the lowering speed, while a hand brake gives manual control of lowering. Wire rope falls must be replaced every four years with certified wire rope. Motor or hand power is used for hoisting these falls, which must be kept coated with a grease that provides lubrication for the internal working of the wire as well as protection against corrosion.

Blocks for both wire and fiber rope must be kept well greased and working easily. An important duty of the crew at lifeboat drills is to see that sheaves for blocks and fairleads work freely.

The decks on which lifeboats are carried must be kept clear of freight or anything else which would interfere with the immediate launching of the lifeboat.

The use of gravity-type davits with electric motor-driven winches has simplified rapid lifeboat launching and hoisting. These almost automatic davits require increased care and skill in their maintenance and routine inspection. Special points to be noted are as follows:

1. *Limit switches*—Before hoisting the boats into the stowed position, check the operation of these devices by pushing down the lever arm to see whether the winch motor stops. Limit switches are in the control or power circuit for the motor. An emergency disconnect switch, which can stop flow of all power to the winch motor, must be manned when the boat is hoisted. Shipmasters must inspect limit switches and emergency disconnect switches every 3 months. Electric motors for lifeboat winches are powerful enough to easily break the wire rope falls if the motor is used to pull up the davit against the stops. This same casualty can occur if air-actuated equipment is used to hoist the davit against the stops. For this reason, the davits should *always* be hand cranked for the last 12 inches or more to their final stowed position.

2. *Winches*—Unless the lubrication schedule for winches is faithfully followed, moisture can accumulate in the winch

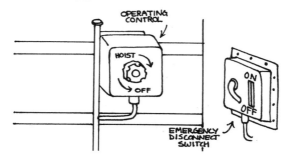

Fig. 17. Lifeboat winch controls.

enclosures to damage wiring and, in cold weather, freeze gears preventing the boat from being lowered. Covers should be fitted over winches to keep ice and snow from freezing on the wire falls.

3. *Hand cranks*—Winch hand cranks have couplings which automatically disengage the crank if the electric motor starts to turn the winch. In order to further reduce any possibility of injury, the emergency disconnect switch should always be in the off position when men are hand cranking.

Lifeboat Operations

Launching. The most difficult operation in handling lifeboats is launching, including embarkation of passengers and crew. To achieve this safely and efficiently, frequent drills are necessary so that each crew member learns his duties and the order in which they must be performed. Training should be so thorough that the crew performs correctly despite any confusion or excitement. For these reasons, weekly drills are required by U.S. laws.

U.S. ships are built to resist damage in an accident. The captain may deem it best for all hands to stay aboard for their own safety and that of the ship. Don't abandon ship before orders are given by the captain or ship's officers.

When using boats handled by mechanical davits, the following would represent a typical sequence of operations necessary to swing the boat over the side:

1. Remove lifeboat cover and its supporting ridgepole. Put cap on drain. Lead sea painter forward, and make fast outboard and clear of all obstructions.

2. Release outboard gripes first so a man assigned to this task cannot be knocked over the side by the swinging of the boat.

3. With falls taut and secured to cleats, cruciform bitts, or winches, release inboard gripes and keel locking lug on chocks.

4. The davits with the boat suspended may now be swung out. Chocks are built high enough above the deck so that if the falls are taut, no hoisting of the boat to clear the deck edge is necessary.

5. When the boat is in outboard position, lower to embarkation deck. With mechanical davits, it is often desirable to swing the davits back inboard so that the boat can be frapped-in snug. This will allow persons to get in the boat without jumping any space between boat and deck.

6. If the ship is pitching as well as rolling, frapping lines should have a fore and aft as well as thwartships lead. With boat complement aboard, davits are again swung outboard. Frapping lines are eased as necessary, and the boat lowered away on falls. In rough weather, the boat crew may have to fend off from ship's side as the ship rolls, and fenders made of mattresses or other available material can be used to cushion impacts.

7. When the boat is in the water, the lifeboatman in charge should turn the releasing gear. The boat can then be held alongside with painter so that men who remained aboard to lower can climb down a ladder into the boat to abandon ship. If the boat cannot be kept alongside because of rough weather, these men can throw heaving lines to the boat; then, with one end secured to themselves, they can get into the water and be pulled aboard the boat.

For boats handled by gravity davits, a different sequence is necessary. This is as follows:

1. Remove boat cover and its supporting ridgepole. Put cap on drain. Lead sea painter forward, and make fast outboard and clear of all obstructions.
2. Release gripes.
3. Raise winch brake handle, and davits with suspended boat should roll to the outboard position. Lower away to embarkation deck. The tricing lines will bring the boat to the side of the ship. The brake should be put on before the tricing lines take all the weight.
4. Before passengers and crew enter the boat at the embarkation deck, frapping lines should be passed and hove taut. With all aboard the boat seated, the hooks on the tricing wires should be released and the boat eased outboard by slacking frapping lines. Releasing the tricing wires without observing these precautions will allow the boat to swing out violently, risking a spill of occupants over the side.

   On some U.S.-flag ships that were built in foreign countries, bowsing tackles may be used instead of frapping lines. These accomplish the same purpose as frapping lines, but are tended from the lifeboat rather than from the embarkation deck of the parent ship. Frequently, two-fold purchases are used. The advantage is that only the brakeman need remain aboard ship when the lifeboat is launched. The disadvantage is that bowsing tackles are cumbersome, and more gear must be stowed in the lifeboat.
5. With the boat in the outboard position, it may be lowered into the water and released. The remaining sequence is similar to that for boats lowered by mechanical davits.

   Picking up a boat at sea can present as many problems as launching it. It is best done by maneuvering to place the boat ahead and to leeward of the ship with the wind about broad on the bow of the ship. If the ship now overtakes the boat with both making way through the water on parallel courses, a sea painter can be passed to the boat. After the painter is fast, the boat's propeller is stopped or oars boated, and then the boat is brought alongside with rudder or steering oar.

The ship can make slow way through the water. If the sea painter is secured well abaft the stem, the tendency to sheer off can be overcome by a strap about the painter from the stem hove close. After the falls are hooked and the boat is hoisted clear of the water, most of the crew can climb the ladder and get aboard the ship; those remaining in the boat should grip the manropes for safety.

On boats handled with gravity davits, the boat is hoisted to a position where the tricing lines can be made fast. It is next lowered to the embarkation deck where men in the boat can get out. It is then brought up to the stowed position, using the hand cranks for the last 12 inches or more. When the boat is back in the stowed position, men can get back in the boat to pass the gripes, replace the ridgepole and cover, and make the boat again secured for sea.

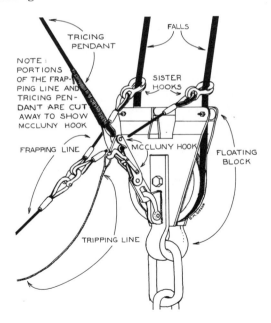

Fig. 18. Tricing pendant and frapping line.

Commands for boats under oars. Commands for boats under oars have not undergone change for many years. A seaman of 100 years ago would be at home in a boat today.

While most commands are addressed to both banks of oars, it may often happen that the coxswain desires to give the command only to one bank, or he may want to give one command to one bank and another command to the other. For example, if it is desired to bring the boat about quickly he may do so by giving the command "give way" to the port bank and "starboard back" to the starboard bank. In any case, it is good policy to call the *bank* first, followed by the command, rather than calling the command followed by the bank that is to execute it. Otherwise one bank may begin to execute a command which is not addressed to it.

When one bank of oars is executing one command and the other bank another and it is desired to give them a command which will apply to both, call "oars" first. This cancels the preceding command and gives both banks an opportunity to start the new order in unison.

Give new commands at the beginning of the stroke, *not* at the end. This gives the oars an opportunity to complete the stroke and execute the new command in unison. The commands and how to execute them are as follows:

1. Stand by the oars—Stroke oar ships his rowlock, clears his oar, and lays in on the gunwale, handle shoved forward to proper position. Immediately, each man back of the stroke oar does the same thing, keeping his oar *inboard* of the oar in front of him.

2. Out oars—Usually given after the command, "Stand by the oars." Oars are placed in rowlocks in the same position as for "oars."

3. Up oars—The oars are tossed quickly to a vertical position, blades trimmed in a fore-and-aft plane and in line with that of the stroke oar, handles of oars resting on bottom boards, outboard hand grasping loom of oar at height of chin, wrist of inboard arm resting on inboard thigh and steadying oar.

4. Toss oars—Complete the stroke and come to "up oars" position. The difference in meaning between this command and "up oars" has disappeared with the passing of time.

5. Shove off—Inboard bowman shoves off smartly from the ship's side with boat hook using the blunt end, shoving the boat ahead, if possible. Outboard bowman takes in the painter. Coxswain sheers off and hauls ahead on the stanchions of the gangway or on the grab rope, assisted as necessary by the inboard stroke oar. Fenders are rigged in by men abreast of them. Bowmen place boat hooks fore and aft, seat themselves, and get their oars ready.

6. Let fall—Given when the boat is clear of the ship's side. As the boat sheers off and away from the ship, it may be necessary to let fall the forward oars before there is room for the after oars to clear the ship's side. This would be done by the command "1, 2, and 3 let fall," or "2 and 3 let fall." Other oars remain vertical until the command "Let fall." At this command all oars are dropped, blades outboard, into the rowlock. Slip the inboard hand to the handle and come to the position "Oars" with both hands on the handle. Under no circumstances should the blades dip water in letting fall.

7. Give way together—All oarsmen take a full stroke, keeping cadence with the stroke oar, *by watching the back of the man in front of them.* Feathering of the oar should become habitual and automatic. If stroke oars have not been able to get their oars out in position by the time the command "give way together" has been given, they will do so quickly and take up the stroke. Continue to pull a strong, steady stroke, using the back, and maintain silence.

8. Hold water—This command is given when way is on the boat and a quick stop is desired. Drop the blades in the water vertically and hold them perpendicular to the keel line. If considerable way is on, especially in a boat that is heavily loaded, care must be used in holding water, or the force of it may carry away the rowlock, gunwale, or the oar itself. Under these conditions, drop the oar in the water at a slight angle, top forward, allowing the water to "slip," and gradually bring the blade vertical as way is lost.

9. Port, hold water (starboard, hold water)—If the boat is under way and the oars rowing, a quick turn may be made by giving this command to one side only, the other side continuing with the command "give way."

10. Stern all—When rowing in ahead motion, complete the stroke, then commence to back water, gradually increasing the depth of immersion of the blades.

11. Back water—Row in astern motion. The difference in meaning between the commands "stern all" and "back water," if any, is now lost with the passage of time. In any event, a good coxswain or boat commander should always give as much warning as possible before giving a new command. He can do this by giving the command, "oars," and then giving the command, "back water." If the boat has any way at all, it is good seamanship to give the command "hold water" first to help take way off the boat. Going from ahead to astern without warning may result in broken rowlocks, rowlocks popped out of their sockets, or an oarsman catching a crab. Sometimes the command "port back water" or "starboard back water" is used when it is desired to come about quickly or turn in close quarters. When this is done the other side can either hold water or give way together.

12. Trail oars—Used in passing obstructions in which the span of the oars would make passing difficult. This command is given when the oars are in the water. Finish the stroke, release the handle of the oar, allowing it to draw fore-and-aft and trail alongside. This command is somewhat awkward to execute, and the oarsman must be careful not to lose his oar. If the boat is in danger of being set down on a dock or other obstruction, oars on that side should be boated to protect them from damage.

13. Bank oars—Used to enable oarsmen to rest their arms when laying to and the position of "oars" would be tiresome to hold. Draw the oar through the rowlock until the handle rests on the opposite gunwale. It is given from the command "oars." The command, "oars across the boat" is sometimes used instead of "bank oars."

14. In bows—Given as landing is approached and while the blades are in the water. Bowmen complete the stroke, toss oars and boat them, seize boat hooks, stand erect in bow, facing forward, holding boat hooks vertical in front of them until they are needed.

15. *Way enough*—Given as the boat approaches for a landing, and takes the place of the two commands "oars" and "boat oars." The command is given at the beginning of a stroke. The stroke is completed, oars tossed to about a 45° angle and boated, forward oar first, stroke oar last. Unship the rowlock. This command may be unnecessary, but can be used to advantage by a good boat commander and a well-trained boat crew.

16. *Oars*—To stop pulling. Given when the coxswain estimates that the boat's headway will carry her to the landing, and while the blades are in the water. Complete the stroke and bring the oars horizontal, at right angles to the keel, blades feathered.

17. *Boat the oars*—Toss the blades to a 45° angle, and lay them inside the boat, blades forward, forward oar first, stroke oar last. Unship the rowlock.

The lifeboat waterborne. After the lifeboat is in the water and the passengers and crew embarked, it is of utmost importance to get the boat clear of the side of the ship as soon as possible. Even in comparatively calm weather the boat can be damaged or personnel injured if the boat stays alongside. If the ship has way on, the boat will clear the side by riding on the sea painter which can then be cast off. If the ship is dead in the water, it may be necessary to fend off by the use of boat hooks or oars. Insure that none of the lines hanging over the side of the vessel foul the propeller or any other part of the boat.

Once clear of the side of the ship, the lifeboat should remain in the vicinity to insure that all survivors are picked up. In the modern day it is extremely unlikely that a ship could sink without shore stations being informed. All ships are now equipped with an EPIRB (Emergency Position-Indicating Radio Beacon), which will float free of the sinking ship and start transmitting signals when the ship goes down. This insures that your position will be known even though the

radio officer has not had time to send an SOS. As a consequence, rescue ships or aircraft will know the ship's position
if survivors stay near the scene of the shipwreck.

The lifeboatman in charge of a boat should try to keep
morale high and to make people in the boat as comfortable
as possible. Signaling equipment should be ready and used
when rescue vessels are sighted or known to be in the
vicinity. Metal objects hoisted as high as possible will help
radar-equipped rescue ships to locate the lifeboat.

Since position is probably known and rescue operations
will shortly be underway, undertaking a long ocean voyage
to the nearest land should be considered only under the most
dire circumstances. Motor lifeboats have fuel only for 24
hours. Attempting to sail or row for a long distance is fool-
hardy. Modern lifeboats are seaworthy, but they are not
meant for sailing. Most of the great lifeboat voyages in
history, such as that of Captain Bligh of *Bounty* fame, were
made in warm water with favorable trade winds helping the
boat towards its destination. In that era, radio, aircraft, and
modern search and rescue procedures were unknown.

Handling propeller-driven boats. Most newer
ships are equipped with either motor-propelled lifeboats or
boats fitted with hand propelling equipment which turns a
propeller. A few merchant ships and all navy ships have
diesel utility boats. The fundamentals of boat handling are
much the same whether a boat is propelled by oars or motor,
and the same boat etiquette must be observed. However,
there are some differences in the maneuverability of the
power-driven boat.

The following basic rules can normally be used as a
foundation for boat handling under power with a right-hand
propeller:

1. Boat stopped, rudder right, engine ahead—bow will
    come right.
2. Boat stopped, rudder left, engine ahead—bow will come
    left.
3. Boat stopped, rudder any direction, engine astern—bow
    will come right. Stern will come left. (No wind situation.)

4. Boat moving astern, rudder left, engine stopped—stern will come left.
5. Boat moving astern, rudder right, engine stopped—stern will come right.
6. Boat moving astern, rudder left, engine ahead—bow will come to left.
7. Boat moving astern, rudder right, engine ahead—bow will come to right.
8. Boat moving ahead, rudder amidships, engine astern—stern will come to left or erratic course.

When using a rudder and propeller, the rudder will have no effect when the boat is not moving unless the propeller is in the ahead position causing a wash over the rudder. Boats with a rudder handle very poorly when going astern. The walking effect of the propeller causes a boat with a right-hand propeller to back to port unless this force is overcome by the tendency to back into the wind. If the boat is moving ahead and the engine is shifted astern, a somewhat erratic course may follow. Experience with a specific boat is required before the actual response can be predicted. Even then, the wind and current must be taken into account, because they affect the track of the boat.

Inflatable Life Rafts

In addition to lifeboats, modern ships are provided with inflatable life rafts. These have replaced the older balsa or Carley life rafts and floats which were in service during World War II and the Korean War. Vessels and tankships that have widely separated accommodations or work areas must have at least one life raft in each such location. Inflatable life rafts have a number of advantages. They are easy to launch; they take up about one-tenth the deck space of a lifeboat of comparable capacity; and, with their proven ability to remain afloat for long periods of time, they provide better survival potential. Disadvantages include limited maneuverability, slow propulsion by paddles, and a propensity to drift because of the boat's lightness.

There are several types of inflatable life rafts on the market, all of which must pass rigid Coast Guard inspection. Depending upon the manufacturer, life rafts have varying characteristics. Some manufacturers provide ladders for boarding. The canopy of one type is rugged enough to permit survivors to jump onto it from the side of the ship. Launching operations also may vary depending upon the particular raft. One example, launching instructions for the RFD Elliott life raft, is shown in figure 19. Because life rafts have different characteristics it is especially important that seamen read carefully the instructions for the life rafts on board their ship before sailing.

The life rafts shown in figures 20 and 21 are typical of those approved by the Coast Guard. The canopy which protects the occupants from cold and dampness is supported by inflatable braces. The towing bridle may be combined with the boarding ladder. The sea anchor, which reduces drift, will keep the head of the raft towards the sea and make it ride more comfortably. The four water pockets fill with water and make the raft more stable. The lifelines on the outside of the raft provide a grip for persons in the water. Similar lifelines on the inside can help the occupants remain in place in severe weather. There is a double floor which can be inflated to help insulate against cold water. A safety knife is provided by the entrance at the end of the raft to cut the painter. The knife cannot cut the fabric of the raft by accident. The raft is designed to catch rainwater to augment the supply of canned water in the raft's original rations. Even so, water should not be issued to occupants for 24 hours. Lights at each end of the canopy operate automatically when raft is launched.

Figure 22 shows the automatic release of the life raft. In the first drawing it is stowed in its cradle on deck. The operating cord must be attached to the cradle, rail, or some part of the ship's structure as shown in figure 20. Should the ship sink so quickly that there is no time to launch the raft, a hydrostatic release will insure that the life raft floats free of the cradle at a depth of about 10 feet. The operating cord is attached to the vessel by a "weak link" which will break if the raft is in danger of being dragged down by the sinking

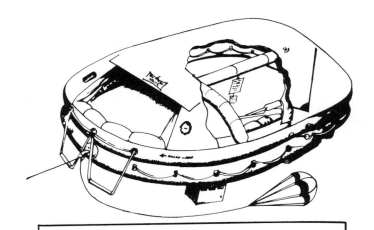

LAUNCHING INSTRUCTIONS

FOR THE

RFD Elliot

INFLATABLE LIFE RAFT

CAUTION

SET FOR OPERATION, DO NOT TAMPER. DO NOT DISTURB METAL BANDS.

1. When stowing raft, always connect the steel link to vessel by shackling painter to cradle using ELLIOT WEAK LINK.

2. Before launching the raft by hand, pull out the painter from the container and make it fast to the cleat provided (on the cradle).

3. If necessary to release painter from cradle, break painter Weak Link manually.

4. Release container by pressing knob on the Hydrostatic Release.

5. Launch life raft complete in container.

6. Gather in painter until taut; give strong pull to inflate raft.

Fig. 19. Drawing of RFD Elliot inflatable life raft and launching instructions. Courtesy RFD Elliot Inc.

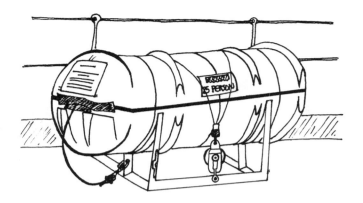

Fig. 20. An inflatable life raft stowed on deck in cradle.

Fig. 21. This inflatable life raft is found on fishing vessels and yachts. Its unique feature is its large ballast chamber which traps water and stabilizes the raft. This raft has withstood typhoons safely. Its capacity is 6 people. Courtesy Givens Associates.

1

The RFD Elliot life raft is secured to its cradle with a hydrostatic release which, if time permits, can be tripped for manual release and inflation of the raft. If time does not permit manual release and inflation, this is accomplished automatically.

2

As the vessel sinks, pressure of the water at a depth of 10 feet actuates the release mechanism, freeing the raft from its stowage. The life raft is inherently buoyant and will float to the surface.

3

The sinking vessel pulls the operating cord and the life raft inflates. The CO_2 gas expands into the buoyancy chambers in a few seconds so that the raft cannot be pulled down by the ship. The sea anchor is streamed automatically when the raft inflates to reduce drift. All rafts are equipped with a spare sea anchor in the emergency equipment.

4

The RFD Weak Link* attaches the painter to the ship; this parts and permits the raft to float free of the sinking vessel. The water-activated light comes on to guide survivors to the raft. Once aboard, help others to board, and then read the raft manual to learn details of raft operation and other data to insure survival.

*Patent pending.

Fig. 22. Automatic release and inflation of life raft. Courtesy RFD Elliot Inc.

vessel. The raft automatically inflates as shown in the third drawing, and is ready to be boarded as shown in the fourth drawing.

Under normal conditions, the life raft is released from the cradle by pressing the knob on the hydrostatic release, carrying it to the rail, and tossing it over the side. The painter is gathered in until taut, and a strong pull on it will start the process of inflating the raft. Although the raft can be inflated on deck, this is not recommended because of the danger of tearing the fabric of the raft when it is manhandled over the side. Should the ship have suffered damage and any sharp edges in holes on the ship's side be present, this could easily happen. Although the raft will float with half its air chambers ruptured and still support its capacity of survivors, there is no point in courting disaster.

Life rafts are provided with an impressive amount of survival equipment: ladder, heaving line, jackknife, lifelines, paddles, sea anchor, towing connections, repair kits, sponges, and bailers. They also contain a survival manual with vital information which should be read by everyone aboard.

Carbon dioxide gas is used to inflate life rafts. Heavy concentrations of this gas can result in unconsciousness leading to death. Therefore, the canopy opening must be adjusted to allow for fresh air. After the raft is inflated, the carbon dioxide exhaled by the survivors will cause some discomfort unless the canopy is kept partially open.

Inflatable life rafts must be inspected by personnel at a certified facility annually. Although rugged, life rafts are designed for one purpose only: to save life. If abused or damaged, they may fail when needed. The fiberglass container is designed to protect the life raft and keep it from the weather. Never tamper with a life raft or any other piece of lifesaving equipment. If a life raft is inflated accidentally, it must be repacked at an approved facility. This is extremely expensive.

Survival Capsules

Some artificial islands and mobile offshore drilling rigs are equipped with survival capsules (fig. 23). The launching mechanism consists of a hold and launch platform, an electric winch, and a single wire rope fall connected to a Rottmer-type hook on top of the capsule. The platform is permanently located so that it extends over the side. Quick launch and recovery operations are possible. Most capsules are equipped with a seawater sprinkling system to provide external fire protection. The capsule is propelled by a diesel engine.

Fig. 23. Survival capsule. Survival capsules are installed on nonself-propelled drilling rigs, self-propelled drilling rigs, fixed structures, and artificial islands. They vary in capacity from 14 to 50 persons. They are launched at the rate of 2 feet per second by a single fall and can make speeds of up to 6 knots. Courtesy Whittaker Corporation.

Personal Flotation Devices

In addition to carrying adequate lifeboats and life rafts, all U.S.-flag vessels must carry at least one Coast Guard approved PFD (personal flotation device) for each person aboard. These must be inspected annually by the Coast Guard, and those which can no longer pass inspection must be replaced. The Type I PFD is the well-known life jacket which comes in adult and child sizes.

The Type IV PFD or ring buoy is not intended to be worn, but is thrown to a person in the water. It is held by the person overboard until rescued. When throwing a ring buoy, throw it near, not at, the person.

The Type V PFD (or workvest) is approved for merchant personnel working near or over the water, but it is not a substitute for the Type I and cannot be counted as a Type I at the annual Coast Guard inspection.

In addition to lifeboats and life rafts, ocean passenger vessels must have life floats or buoyant apparatus for emergency use by the passengers. These must be stowed for quick launchings with lashings capable of being easily cast off. Unless skids are provided, buoyant apparatus and life floats must weigh less than 400 pounds to insure easy launching and are provided with a boat hook, paddles, waterlights, painter, and lifeline.

Immersion Suits

In addition to being able to float, a person in the water must stay warm enough to avoid losing body heat and suffering from the resulting hypothermia. An immersion suit is now required for each passenger or crew member on every U.S.-flag vessel that operates in cold offshore waters or in harsh and remote regions.

These suits are constructed primarily of a closed-cell flexible foam that meets buoyancy and thermal insulation requirements. They must fit properly and form a tight seal around the face. They have light reflective material, and are colored what the Coast Guard calls "vivid reddish green."

The wearer's head is maintained above the surface of the water, and the suit must be capable of turning over an unconscious person so that his mouth is clear of the water within five seconds. In addition, the wearer must be able to suit up in two minutes. The suit's zipper should be lubricated regularly with paraffin so that it works easily, and the suit should be stowed where it is handy.

Survival suits are both bulky and cumbersome, but they work! You should practice donning your suit before an emergency. Make sure yours fits and is in good condition. The place to put it on is topside, not below decks where it may hamper you in getting to your abandon ship station.

Global Maritime Distress and Safety System (GMDSS)

All large oceangoing vessels are provided with lifeboat radios which are carried to a lifeboat for drills or when actually abandoning ship. Gone are the bulky lifeboat emergency radios that were hand cranked for power while another person sent an SOS message with a telegraph key. Now, a vessel's

Fig. 24. Immersion suit familiarization aboard T.S. *Golden Bear*. Courtesy Midn. Brian Goldman, California Maritime Academy.

GMDSS survival craft equipment includes emergency position indicating radio beacons (EPIRBs), search and rescue transponders (SARTs) and portable very high frequency (VHF) radios. The EPIRB will signal passing satellites that you are in distress and automatically send your position to rescue centers. As the rescue vessels or aircraft close in on your position, your SART will indicate your exact position on their search radars. Finally, as you hear or see the approaching rescue craft, you can talk to them on your VHF radio to assist in your recovery.

Morse Code

Although manually keyed distress signals in lifeboats are a thing of the past, the editors cannot recommend too strongly that anyone who earns his or her living at sea learn the Morse Code. This is only required for licensed deck officers, but in an emergency situation, a seaman who could talk to a rescue ship by flashing light might play a key role in a rescue operation.

For manual keying in the transmission and reception of messages, the Morse Code is given below:

A ·—	J ·———	S ···	2 ··———
B —···	K —·—	T —	3 ···——
C —·—·	L ·—··	U ··—	4 ····—
D —··	M ——	V ···—	5 ·····
E ·	N —·	W ·——	6 —····
F ··—·	O ———	X —··—	7 ——···
G ——·	P ·——·	Y —·——	8 ———··
H ····	Q ——·—	Z ——··	9 ————·
I ··	R ·—·	1 ·————	0 —————

Distress Signals

The following distress signals, contained in Annex IV, 72 COLREGS (International Regulations for Preventing Collision at Sea), are recognized by all maritime nations:

1. Need of assistance. The following signals, used or exhibited either together or separately, indicate distress and need of assistance:

(a) a gun or other explosive signal fired at intervals of about a minute;

(b) a continuous sounding with any fog-signaling apparatus;

(c) rockets or shells, throwing red stars fired one at a time at short intervals;

(d) a signal made by radiotelegraphy or by any other signaling method consisting of the group ... — — — ... (SOS) in the Morse Code;

(e) a signal sent by radiotelephony consisting of the spoken word "Mayday";

(f) the International Code Signal of distress indicated by N.C.;

(g) a signal consisting of a square flag having above or below it a ball or anything resembling a ball;

(h) flames on the vessel (as from a burning tar barrel, oil barrel, etc.);

(i) a rocket parachute flare or a hand flare showing a red light;

(j) a smoke signal giving off orange-colored smoke;

(k) slowly and repeatedly raising and lowering arms outstretched to each side;

(l) the radiotelegraph alarm signal;

(m) the radiotelephone alarm signal;

(n) signals transmitted by emergency position-indicating radio beacons.

2. The use or exhibition of any of the foregoing signals except for the purpose of indicating distress and need of assistance and the use of other signals which may be confused with any of the above signals is prohibited.

3. Attention is drawn to the relevant sections of the International Code of Signals, the *Merchant Ship Search and Rescue Manual*, and the following signals:

(a) a piece of orange-colored canvas with either a black square and circle or other appropriate symbol (for identification from the air);

(b) a dye marker.

I Landing signals for the guidance of small boats with crews or persons in distress

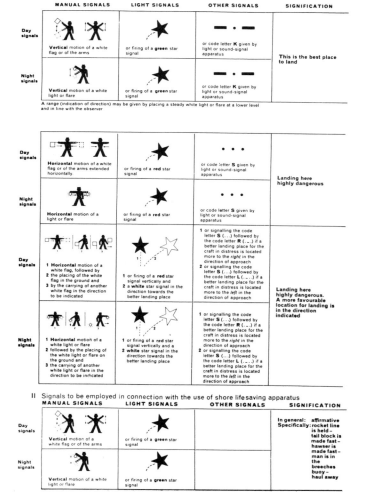

II Signals to be employed in connection with the use of shore lifesaving apparatus

Fig. 25. Table of Lifesaving Signals. Courtesy Defense Mapping Agency Hydrographic Center.

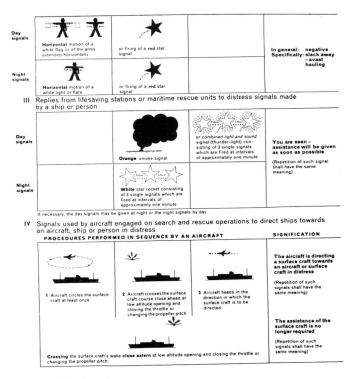

| Day signals | Horizontal motion of a white flag or of the arms extended horizontally | or firing of a red star signal | | In general: negative
Specifically: slack away
– avast
hauling |
| Night signals | Horizontal motion of a white light or flare | or firing of a red star signal | | |

III Replies from lifesaving stations or maritime rescue units to distress signals made by a ship or person

| Day signals | Orange smoke signal | or combined *light and sound* signal (thunder-light) consisting of 3 single signals which are fired at intervals of approximately one minute | You are seen – assistance will be given as soon as possible

(Repetition of such signal shall have the same meaning) |
| Night signals | | White star rocket consisting of 3 single signals which are fired at intervals of approximately one minute | |

If necessary, the day signals may be given at night or the night signals by day

IV Signals used by aircraft engaged on search and rescue operations to direct ships towards an aircraft, ship or person in distress

PROCEDURES PERFORMED IN SEQUENCE BY AN AIRCRAFT			SIGNIFICATION
1 Aircraft circles the surface craft at least once	2 Aircraft crosses the surface craft course close ahead at low altitude opening and closing the throttle or changing the propeller pitch	3 Aircraft heads in the direction in which the surface craft is to be directed	The aircraft is directing a surface craft towards an aircraft or surface craft in distress (Repetition of such signals shall have the same meaning)
	Crossing the surface craft's wake **close astern** at low altitude opening and closing the throttle or changing the propeller pitch		The assistance of the surface craft is no longer required (Repetition of such signals shall have the same meaning)

Fig. 25—*Continued*

Landing on a Beach

Although the lifesaving signals given above provide for communication between the boat crew and beach personnel, landing through heavy surf is highly dangerous and should not be attempted. Lifeboats are not surfboats. Beamy lifeboats or rafts handle poorly in the surf and will easily broach or capsize. Survivors in lifeboats are well advised to wait for rescue by helicopter or other rescue craft. Beach landings

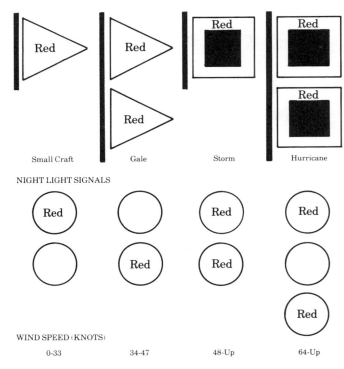

Fig. 26. Storm warning signals. Whenever winds dangerous to navigation are forecast for an area, the signals shown above may be hoisted. The signals indicate that the mariner can expect these weather conditions within the next 12 hours.

should be attempted only in an extreme emergency. However, if beaching through surf is absolutely necessary to save life or limb, the following procedures are generally recommended:

1. Boats under oars should be landed with the bow to the sea. Remember that surf always looks less severe from seaward. This allows better control by the coxswain using his sweep oar to assist in keeping the bow to the sea. A sea anchor can be used from the bow to assist in

Fig. 27. Manual distress signal for daytime use. The signal illustrated in the drawing is made by slowly and repeatedly raising and lowering the arms outstretched to each side. This signal is simple, needing no special equipment. The visibility of the signal is improved by holding in each hand a handkerchief, towel, bathing suit, or other attention-getting material.

controlling the boat. In between swells, back water to move the boat closer to the beach. *Do not rush this operation.* Disembark all hands immediately when the boat lands.

2. Power boats or Fleming gear propelled boats may normally be landed best by using the available oars and landing in the same way as a boat under oars. However, this requires persons who are physically fit and well trained.

3. If a power boat must be landed under propeller power, a bow first landing is usually the only feasible way. A sea anchor should be towed astern to assist maneuvering. Landing a power boat is *not* recommended under any circumstances.

4. Life rafts have minimum control, so beaching through surf is extremely hazardous and should be avoided. If beaching becomes inevitable or is required in an emergency, take advantage of wind and sea. Avoid rocky areas if possible and keep all weight low in the raft to avoid capsizing. All hands should disembark as soon as

the raft grounds, and the raft should be pulled up to the high water mark.

Rescue of a Person Overboard and Survivors in the Water

At the first cry of "man overboard," a ring buoy should be thrown to mark the spot and to give the person something with which to keep afloat if possible. The rudder should be turned in the direction of the person to prevent the propeller from striking him. In the daytime a smoke distress signal will help mark the position of the victim overboard, whereas at night a flare or water light attached to the ring buoy will serve the same purpose.

At all cost, the person overboard should be kept in sight. Someone on board should be directed to do this and perform no other duty. If the person can be kept in sight, a circle recovery maneuver is the quickest way to bring the victim back aboard in daytime. Recovery of a person by ship or by lifeboat will depend upon the weather and other factors.

At night the Williamson turn is the best means of bringing the overboard victim aboard even though it takes somewhat longer than a circle recovery. To execute the Williamson turn, the rudder is put over hard towards the side from which the man has fallen overboard. The rudder is continued full until the ship is 60° from the original heading, and then shifted full to the opposite direction. The ship continues to turn in the new direction until steadied up on the opposite (or reciprocal) of the original course. When the ship is on the reciprocal course, the man should be close aboard the bow on the side from which he fell.

The approach to a person who is to be picked up in the water is much like the approach to a landing with the added factor that the victim will drift to leeward with the wind and sea while a dock or pier will not.

The parent ship should be to windward of and as close as possible to the victim when the boat is put in the water, in order to reduce the time the victim will have to spend in the

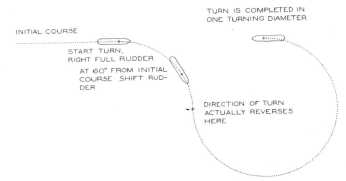

Fig. 28. The Williamson turn.

boat, as well as to shorten the trip the boat will make to pick up the individual in the open ocean.

The most important factor is the safety of the boat, because a swamped boat will be of no use to the individual in the water. Whether the approach is made from leeward or windward of the individual will depend upon the circumstances. If the victim overboard is to leeward, then approach from the lee; if to windward, approach from windward. The bowmen should boat their oars a few lengths off and point in the direction of the victim to assist the boat commander in the final approach. The victim should be picked up as carefully and gently as possible. The victim may be injured, in a state of shock, or irrational. Therefore, a member of the boat crew should be detailed to tend the victim on the way back to the ship. Voice radio contact between the boat and the ship is very helpful.

Helicopter Evacuation

Helicopter evacuation for merchant ship personnel requiring urgent medical assistance is available in many areas of the world. This is a hazardous undertaking on the part of the helicopter pilot and his crew and requires both cooperation and good seamanship on the part of the merchant ship. The

Coast Guard requires that instructions for this maneuver be posted in the pilothouse of all vessels. Read them! Some of the most important points are:

1. Do *not* shine any lights on the helicopter at night.
2. Have the hoist area clear of obstructions. Area should have at least a 50-foot radius.
3. Patient should be as close to hoist area as possible and ready for transfer.
4. Basket or stretcher should touch deck prior to handling to avoid shock.
5. Do *not* secure cable from helicopter to vessel.
6. Master should choose course so that wind is on the bow and stack gases are clear of the hoist area.

Sample Multiple-Choice Questions
for Lifeboatman Examination

The lifeboatman examination given by the Coast Guard consists of a written and a practical test. The written test poses 70 multiple-choice questions. The sample which follows has been taken from published banks of questions which the Coast Guard uses in preparing questions for use in the examining room. The prospective lifeboatman is cautioned that sometimes a few able seaman questions may turn up on the lifeboatman exam. Similarly, lifeboatman questions may turn up on the able seaman exam. So the wise applicant will not try to "get by" by studying as little as possible. Simply knowing the answers to the questions given here won't do. Roll up your sleeves and wade in with both feet. The letter of the correct answer to each question is set in boldface type.

1. The way to operate the hand-held distress flare is to:
    a. remove cap and pull ignitor wire
    b. remove cap and scratch handle on hard object
    c. remove cap and scratch button on flare against the surface on the cap
    d. turn cap clockwise

2. Who should test and inspect an inflatable life raft?
   a. Chief Mate
   b. qualified sales and service representative
   c. shipyard personnel
   d. certified lifeboatman

3. Inflatable life rafts are provided with:
   a. a Very pistol
   b. a towing connection
   c. a portable radio
   d. canned milk

4. Life rafts must be overhauled and inspected at least every:
   a. 6 months
   b. 12 months
   c. 18 months
   d. 24 months

5. The purpose of underwater pockets on a life raft is to:
   a. store rain water
   b. stabilize the raft
   c. stow life raft equipment
   d. aid in righting the raft if it inflates upside down

6. Where is the sheath knife in a life raft located?
   a. in the first aid kit
   b. on a line hanging down from the canopy
   c. in the equipment bag
   d. in a pocket on the edge of the raft

7. The primary purpose of the hydrostatic release on a life raft is to:
   a. inflate the life raft
   b. test the pressure in the raft
   c. hold raft on its cradle
   d. release the raft if the vessel sinks

8. How do you hand launch a life raft?
   a. pull a cord
   b. cut metal restraining bands
   c. remove elastic packing strap
   d. throw the container overboard

9. The best way to release a life raft from its cradle is by:
   a. cutting the metal straps
   b. the screw turnbuckle on the back of the cradle
   c. lifting one end of the raft
   d. pushing the plunger on the center of the hydrostatic release

10. A life raft should be manually released from its cradle by:
    a. cutting the straps
    b. Rottmer Release
    c. Static release
    d. Hydrostatic release-pushing plunger

11. What position should a person assume if in the sea wearing a life jacket for an extended period of time?
    a. assume spar position; legs extended down, arms spread
    b. legs and arms spread apart lying on back
    c. knees tucked up to chin
    d. lying on stomach face underwater except for breathing

12. A ship's abandon ship signal is:
    a. 6 short blasts and 1 long blast
    b. 1 long for 10 seconds
    c. more than 6 short blasts and 1 long blast
    d. 6 short blasts, more than 1 long blast

13. The lights on the outside of the canopy of an inflatable life raft operate:
    a. by turning on a switch located inside the canopy
    b. only at night

c. light sensor
d. automatically

14. When lowering the life raft by hand, what operation should take place?
    a. operating cord detaches automatically
    b. operating cord should be attached to some substantial part of the ship
    c. you should open casing by cutting metal straps
    d. you should inflate the raft on deck first

15. Which operation should be done when launching a portable life raft?
    a. open red valve on CO_2 apparatus
    b. secure operating cord to the vessel
    c. after inflation, detach operation cord from life raft
    d. open life raft casing

16. When a life raft is launched, the operating cord is used for:
    a. a sea painter
    b. cut out and thrown away
    c. to secure the boarding ladder
    d. an emergency fishing line

17. When in a life raft in very cold weather, the greatest danger is:
    a. sharks
    b. freezing
    c. danger of CO_2 from keeping canopy closed
    d. starvation

18. The inflatable bottom on the life raft is to protect you from cold and:
    a. CO_2 asphyxiation
    b. warm water
    c. rough water
    d. to keep the sides of the raft full of air

19. The purpose of oil in the sea anchor is:
    a. to weigh down the anchor
    b. to lubricate the anchor
    c. to repel dangerous fish
    d. to help smooth the sea

20. The operating cord of an inflatable life raft is also used as:
    a. tow line
    b. painter
    c. orange smoke flares
    d. lifeline

21. When reaching ashore in a life raft, the *first* thing to do is:
    a. secure the life raft for possible use as a shelter
    b. go get some firewood
    c. remove the provisions from the life raft
    d. abandon the life raft and send it out to sea in hopes that someone will spot it

22. Signaling device provided in the inflatable life raft is:
    a. Very pistol
    b. orange smoke flares
    c. air horn
    d. lantern

23. The floor of the life raft can be inflated by:
    a. launching raft overboard pull cord
    b. hand pump in tool bag
    c. extra CO_2 canisters for floor
    d. bleeding air out of the sides

24. To haul a life raft back on board, you should:
    a. hook line to eye on raft
    b. pass lines under the raft
    c. hook line to towing bridles
    d. deflate the raft

25. When using the hand held type signaling mirror, one hand is used to hold the mirror and the other:
    a. is held behind the mirror
    b. is held in front of the mirror
    c. used to shield the eyes
    d. used to shield the mirror

26. When lowering boat during rough weather it is advisable to:
    a. avoid the use of frapping lines as it may endanger the boat
    b. lower the boat near the water and have crew board using embarkation ladder
    c. release tricing pendant before removing boat from cradle
    d. have heaving line ready and standing by

27. You are in a raft, drifting at sea, which of the following is an indication of land nearby?
    a. fog
    b. cumulus clouds
    c. birds
    d. flying fish

28. The tricing pendant should be released:
    a. before the boat is lowered
    b. before the passengers get in
    c. after the passengers get in
    d. after the boat is afloat

29. If you are headed 270° True in a life raft, you are going:
    a. north
    b. south
    c. east
    d. west

30. Life rafts are less maneuverable than lifeboats due to their weight, shallow draft and:
    a. large number of appurtenances

   b. large sail area
   c. greater amount of equipment
   d. inability to withstand heavy seas

31. If the inflatable life raft is to be taken in tow, the tow-
    line is to be connected to the:
    a. towing connection (bridle)
    b. life line
    c. boarding ladder
    d. all of the above

32. Which of the following would help to survive an ex-
    tended period in a life raft?
    a. wet clothing to prevent the body from dehydration
    b. keep the raft pumped up as hard as possible
    c. keep busy
    d. all of the above

33. The error in a magnetic compass caused by the vessel's
    magnetism is called:
    a. variation
    b. deviation
    c. compass error
    d. bearing error

34. The lever for the mechanical disengaging apparatus on
    a lifeboat shall be marked by:
    a. painting the lever white
    b. painting the area around the lever red
    c. the words "Danger Lever Lowers Boat"
    d. painting the lever red

35. Water should not be issued to occupants (healthy peo-
    ple) of a life raft for:
    a. 8 hours
    b. 10 hours
    c. 24 hours
    d. 48 hours

36. BOTH INTERNATIONAL AND INLAND Which signal, other than a distress signal, can be used by a vessel to attract attention?
    a. searchlight beam
    b. continuous sounding of a fog signal apparatus
    c. burning barrel
    d. orange smoke signal

37. The command, in a boat under oars, to complete the stroke and place oars in the boat:
    a. oars
    b. way enough
    c. hold water
    d. in bows

38. When a sea anchor is used in landing in a heavy surf, headway is checked by:
    a. slacking the tripping line and towing the apex end forward
    b. slacking the tripping line and towing the mouth forward by the holding line
    c. towing with the tripping line and the holding line slack
    d. towing the apex end forward with the tripping line

39. The floating orange smoke signal is ignited:
    a. automatically by water
    b. by a small pull wire
    c. by striking the cap on the striker bottom
    d. by lighting a match

40. If you must swim through an oil fire, you should NOT:
    a. wear as much clothing as possible
    b. enter the water feet first
    c. swim with the wind
    d. cover eyes with one hand when entering the water

41. The purpose of air tanks in a lifeboat is to:
    a. help the lifeboat float

b. add strength to the lifeboat
c. keep lifeboat afloat if boat becomes flooded
d. put in provisions

42. When first using the compass in a lifeboat you must be careful to:
    a. be sure to mount it on the centerline of the boat
    b. add western variation to error
    c. disregard deviation because the lifeboat is so small compared to the ship
    d. check compass for error at noon

43. An immersion suit must be equipped with a(n):
    a. air bottle for breathing
    b. whistle and light
    c. whistle, light, and reflective tape
    d. whistle, light, and sea dye marker

44. Most enclosed lifeboats will right themselves after capsizing IF the:
    a. lowest ballast tanks are filled with water
    b. fuel tanks are not less than half full
    c. passengers are strapped to their seats
    d. sea anchor is deployed to windward

45. Which primarily functions as a support?
    a. limber hole
    b. thwart
    c. stanchion
    d. footing

46. What is the length of the heaving line on an inflatable life raft?
    a. 10 fathoms
    b. 15 fathoms
    c. 20 fathoms
    d. 25 fathoms

47. The greatest hazard to survival of a person in the sea is:
    a. weakening of the muscles due to wave action
    b. muscle cramps
    c. exposure to sun and wind
    d. loss of body heat

48. The most commonly used davit on merchant vessels to-day is:
    a. radial
    b. sheath screw
    c. gravity
    d. quadrantal

49. Limit switches must be tested at least once every:
    a. week
    b. month
    c. 2 months
    d. 3 months

50. The grab rail of a metal lifeboat is normally located:
    a. along the turn of the bilge
    b. along each side of the keel
    c. near the top of the gunwale
    d. at the bow and at the stern

51. What is the most important thing to check before lowering a boat?
    a. oars
    b. life jackets
    c. sea painter
    d. boat plug

52. One short blast of the whistle means:
    a. secure lifeboats
    b. raise boats
    c. lower boats
    d. drill is over

53. When lowering a lifeboat to the embarkation deck, which of the following are used to bring the boat to the side of the ship?
    a. pull lines
    b. boat hooks
    c. tricing pendants
    d. frapping line

54. The canopy of an inflatable life raft should:
    a. go into place as the raft is inflated
    b. be put up after everyone is aboard
    c. be put up only in severe weather
    d. be used as a sail if the wind is blowing

55. When operating the air supply system in a covered lifeboat, the:
    a. fuel supply valve should be closed
    b. hatches, doors, and oar ports should be closed
    c. air cylinder shut-off valve should be closed
    d. engine should be shut off

56. The boat command meaning "complete the stroke, stop rowing, and hold blades flat" is:
    a. "Oars"
    b. "Up oars"
    c. "Way enough"
    d. "Hold water"

57. After launching an inflatable raft should be kept dry inside by:
    a. opening the automatic drain plugs
    b. draining the water pockets
    c. using the electric bilge pump
    d. using the bailers and cellulose sponge

58. Lines passed around the falls to hold the boat while passengers are boarding are:
    a. life lines
    b. frapping lines

c. tricing lines
d. tripping lines

59. Inflatable liferafts are provided with a:
    a. jackknife
    b. towing connection
    c. lifeline
    d. all of the above

60. If the coxswain of your lifeboat gives the command "Hold Water" you should:
    a. complete the stroke, raise your oar slightly, swinging the oar slightly forward, and place it in the boat
    b. lift the oar into a vertical position
    c. used to enable oarsmen to rest their arms after a long row
    d. dip the blade of your oar into the water vertically and hold it perpendicular to the keel line

61. Inflatable liferafts are provided with:
    a. portable radio
    b. oil lantern
    c. canned milk
    d. towing bridle

62. The purpose of the wire stretched between the davit heads is to:
    a. keep the movements of the davits at the same speed
    b. keep the davits from slipping when they are in the stowed position
    c. prevent vibration during lowering of the boat
    d. support the man-ropes

63. The falls on gravity davits are:
    a. manila
    b. nylon
    c. wire
    d. any of the above

64. A person has fallen overboard and is being picked up
    with a lifeboat. If the person appears in danger of
    drowning, the lifeboat should be maneuvered to make:
    a. an approach from leeward
    b. a direct approach
    c. the most direct approach
    d. an approach from across wind

65. When a man who has fallen overboard is being picked
    up by a lifeboat, the boat should approach with the wind:
    a. astern and the victim just off the bow
    b. ahead and the victim just off the bow
    c. just off the bow and the victim to windward
    d. just off the bow and the victim to leeward

66. When evacuating a seaman by helicopter life, the vessel
    should be:
    a. stopped with the wind dead ahead
    b. stopped with the wind on the beam
    c. underway with the wind 30 degrees on the bow
    d. underway on a course to provide no apparent wind

67. You have abandoned ship and find yourself aboard a
    lifeboat in a heavy sea. Your boat is able to make way
    through the water. To prevent broaching you should:
    a. put the sea on your stern and run as fast as the boat
       will go
    b. take no action to prevent broaching as this is recom-
       mended maneuver in a heavy sea
    c. head boat into swells to take them at a 30 to 40 de-
       gree angle on either bow, run as slow as possible
       without losing steerage
    d. place everyone as far forward as possible to keep the
       boat "bow heavy"

68. Which of the following davit types may be operated by
    one man?
    a. quadrantal
    b. gravity

    c. sheath-screw
    d. radial

69. Where should the station bills be posted?
    a. crew's quarters area
    b. dining area
    c. vessel control room
    d. all of the above

70. Fire and abandon ship stations and duties may be found on the:
    a. crewman's duty list
    b. certificate of inspection
    c. shipping articles
    d. station bill

71. In rough weather, when a ship is able to maneuver, it is best to launch a lifeboat:
    a. on the lee side
    b. on the windward side
    c. with the wind ahead
    d. with the wind from astern

72. When a ship is abandoned and there are several rafts in the water, one of the first things to be done is:
    a. separate the rafts as much as possible to increase chances of detection
    b. transfer all supplies to one raft
    c. transfer all the injured to one raft
    d. secure the rafts together to keep them from drifting apart

73. While at your lifeboat station, you hear a signal consisting of two short blasts of the whistle. This indicates:
    a. abandon ship
    b. commence lowering boats
    c. stop lowering boats
    d. secure from boat stations

74. Which of the following is *not* required by law to be posted aboard a vessel?
    a. Certificate of Inspection
    b. Official Crew List
    c. officer's licenses
    d. Station Bill

75. What is meant by the term "two blocked?"
    a. The bottom block touches the top block.
    b. The line has jumped the sheaves.
    c. There are turns in the fall.
    d. You have two blocks.

76. A "bowline" is used to:
    a. join lines of equal size
    b. form a temporary eye (loop) in the end of a line
    c. be a stopper
    d. keep a line from fraying

77. When evacuating a seaman by helicopter lift, which of the following statements is true?
    a. The vessel should be stopped with the wind dead ahead during the hoisting operation.
    b. Flags should be flown to provide a visual reference as to the direction of the apparent wind.
    c. The drop line should be grounded first then secured as close to the hoist point as possible.
    d. The hoist area should be located as far aft as possible so the pilot will have a visual reference while approaching.

78. Safety equipment on board vessels must be approved by the:
    a. Coast Guard
    b. Safety Standards Bureau
    c. Occupational Health & Safety Agency (OSHA)
    d. National Safety Council

79. While underway in thick fog you are on watch and hear the cry "Man Overboard." What would you expect the watch officer to do?
    a. Be sure the man is clear, back down until stopped, then send a boat
    b. round turn
    c. race track turn
    d. Williamson turn

80. Which of the following statements about the Williamson turn is false?
    a. It requires the highest degree of shiphandling skills to accomplish.
    b. It is the slowest of methods used in turning the vessel.
    c. It is the best turn to use when the victim is not in sight due to reduced visibility.
    d. It returns the vessel to the original trackline on a reciprocal course.

81. When a sea anchor for a lifeboat is properly rigged, it will do which of the following?
    a. Prevent the lifeboat from drifting.
    b. Help to prevent broaching
    c. Prevent the lifeboat from pitching.
    d. None of the above.

82. What word is an international distress signal when sent by radiotelephone?
    a. Securité
    b. Mayday
    c. Breaker
    d. Pan

83. The master shall insure that each deck from which lifeboats are launched is:
    a. surfaced with a nonskid texture
    b. roped off to prevent unnecessary access
    c. kept clear of any obstructions that would interfere with launching

d. posted with a list of persons assigned to the lifeboat

84. When may a work vest be substituted for a required life preserver?
    a. To replace a damaged life preserver
    b. For use during fire drills
    c. For use during boat drills
    d. At no time

85. What does "EPIRB" stand for?
    a. Emergency Position Indicating Radar Buoy
    b. Electronic Pulse Indicating Radiobeacon
    c. Emergency Position Indicating Radiobeacon
    d. None of the above

86. Preparation of Station Bills and signing of same is the responsibility of the:
    a. chief officer of the vessel
    b. owner of the vessel
    c. master of the vessel
    d. United States Coast Guard

87. Which statement is TRUE concerning lifesaving equipment?
    a. The master may assign an officer to keep the lifesaving equipment in good condition.
    b. All lifeboat winch control apparatuses are required to be examined every month.
    c. Nothing may be stowed in a lifeboat other than the required equipment.
    d. All of the above.

88. A placard containing instructions for use of the breeches buoy (Form CG-811) shall be placed:
    a. in the pilothouse and engine room
    b. in the messroom(s)
    c. where available to the watch officer
    d. where best visible in the officer's and crew's quarters

2. Fire

All seamen must be conscious of the danger of fire and should continuously update their knowledge and skills in fire prevention, fire detection, and fire fighting. The risk of fire at sea is always present, and the results of fire are too often tragic. A study of the fires aboard the *Morro Castle, Lakonia,* and *Prinsendam* is very sobering and educational. The brief treatment of fire in this book sketches only those aspects pertaining to control and extinguishment as well as fighting various kinds of fire. For those who wish a more complete study, the reader is directed to the U.S. Maritime Administration's manual, *Marine Fire Prevention, Firefighting, and Fire Safety* from which the material in this text has been taken.

Elements of Fire and Its Control

Although fire is a complex phenomenon, it consists basically of four parts or components, which are fuel, heat, oxygen, and a chain reaction, as shown in figure 29. The control and extinguishment of ordinary fires in general is brought about by eliminating any one of the components. If oxygen (air) can be diluted or smothered out, the flame will go out. If heat can be taken away by cooling the fuel to a temperature below that at which it will take fire, then the fire can no longer exist. If the chain reaction can be interrupted, flame and heat cannot be formed; therefore, there will be no fire. For the purposes of this manual, it is assumed aboard ship that, except in rare cases, it will be impossible to remove the fuel from the heat and the oxygen in order to put the fire out.

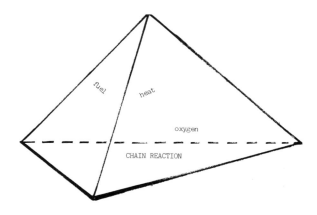

Fig. 29. Elements of fire—the fire tetrahedron. Although sometimes described as the "fire triangle," the term "fire tetrahedron," or four-sided figure, is a better explanation of the nature of fire. Fuel, heat, and oxygen can be considered the sides of the figure, and the base is the chain reaction or combustion. If any one of the sides of the figure is lacking, the tetrahedron will not be complete and will fall apart. There will be no chain reaction.

Therefore, the task of the fire fighter will be to reduce the temperature (to cool the fire), to isolate the fire from its supply of oxygen (to smother the fire), or to interrupt the chain reaction, and to accomplish these with the greatest possible speed.

Transmission of heat. Heat may be transmitted in three ways: by radiation, by conduction, and by convection. Through radiation heat is transmitted in direct rays, equally in all directions. Decks and bulkheads are heated by radiation. The heat passes through them by conduction to ignite combustibles on the opposite side, either directly by conduction or by radiation and convection.

Conduction is the process in which the molecules of a substance are heated by molecules having a higher temperature with which they are in contact. The rate of heat transfer by conduction varies with the substance. Some substances conduct heat more readily than others. Steel bulkheads are excellent conductors, and will remain unaffected while transmitting heat to dangerous combustibles.

In convection, portions of gases and liquids that are heated to a higher temperature than the rest of their mass become lighter in weight and move upward into the cooler portions above. It is by convection that heated air and other heated gases rise over a fire and are carried by the wind to ignite combustibles at some distance away. This process is particularly applicable to ventilation systems aboard ships, which may carry the heated gases to places far removed from the fire.

Removal of fuel. When dealing with the removal of the fuel, the fire fighter on board ship must take whatever measures possible to prevent additional fuel from coming into contact with the fire since he cannot, in most cases, entirely separate the combustibles from the fire. Fire fighters must be ready at all times to shift combustibles to safe areas. Jettisoning deck cargo in danger of catching fire and shutting off valves to stop the flow of liquid fuel to a fire are elementary precautions.

Removal of heat. Another method of extinguishing fire is to deal with the second component—heat. Normally, the best way to remove heat is by the use of water and water sprays and by ventilating to outside areas, except in a compartment where it is possible to close off openings and thus smother the fire.

Removal or control of air (oxygen). The third component of fire—air—is difficult to control. Usually it is practically impossible to remove air from the atmosphere surrounding the fire. However, it can be diluted with other gases which are noncombustible, such as CO_2 (carbon dioxide), or excluded (smothered) with foam, so that extinguishment of the fire will occur.

Removing the supply of oxygen and cooling the blazing substance below those temperatures where fire occurs are the most useful methods of stopping fire. In cargo holds, oxygen is kept out by closing all openings to the atmosphere.

Ventilation is stopped, hatches and manholes battened down, and oxygen present is displaced or diluted with CO_2 or steam.

Most modern ships are fitted with CO_2 extinguishing systems. CO_2 is a gas which will not ordinarily support combustion. It will not support human life. Engine rooms fitted with CO_2 extinguishing systems have alarm bells caused to ring by the gas as it is released. When these bells sound, all personnel in the space should get out. In holds or other spaces, men should be warned to get out before CO_2 is released.

Because CO_2 is an inert gas, it does not readily react with materials to change their properties. CO_2 does not damage cargo in a hold, as steam or water might. Aside from its hazard to personnel, its principal drawback is that only a limited quantity is available aboard ship. This requires that the space afire be kept closed off and the gas be used carefully. Vessels fitted with CO_2 systems usually have a chart on the bridge and in the CO_2 room. These set forth the number of bottles to release in order to inert the atmosphere of any specific area of the ship against fire.

Because the gas in the CO_2 bottles is kept under a pressure of up to 2000 pounds per square inch, such bottles should be handled with care and their temperature kept below 130° Fahrenheit. CO_2 is heavier than air and is the familiar "dry ice" in its solid form. In the open air, dry ice goes directly to a gas, but under the high pressure in the cylinder it exists as a liquid. When released, it forms particles of dry ice from the cooling effect of expansion. Human skin can be "burned" by the intense cold as this gas is released from under pressure.

In older ships a steam-smothering system may be installed in the engineering spaces. If installed, steam is used in much the same manner as CO_2. Because of condensation more steam is required than CO_2, and it has been found to be less effective. For this reason, it is no longer approved for installation in newly constructed American-flag vessels.

Controlling chain reactions. Although the actions of certain extinguishing dusts, powders, or finely divided dry chemicals are not fully understood, sufficient work has been done to indicate that the vapors from burning substances progress through a chain of chemical reactions. Therefore, the introduction of an inhibiting powder is able to break the progress from link to link of the chain so that the chemical reactions which result in the fire stop. A commonly used chemical inhibitor has been Halon, but it is being phased out because of environmental considerations. No new installations are being authorized, but existing ones can be utilized.

Halon can be used for:

Class A fires if not deep seated
Class B fires
Class C fires
Fires in storage areas where articles of high value may be damaged by residue from other agents.

Ignition temperature. The ignition temperature of a substance is the lowest temperature at which its vapor, usually a gas generated through the application of heat, will ignite independently of any external source of ignition. A substance or its vapor, however, does not have to be heated to its ignition temperature throughout in order for it to be ignited with an external source of ignition.

Petroleum oils ignite, without any external source of ignition, at 490° F. to 765° F., which is several hundred degrees higher than their "flash points"; butter and cooking greases ignite at 650° F. to 750° F. and "flash" at lower temperatures; wood ignites at 450° to 520° F. Each substance has different "fire" and "flash points," neither of which has any relationship to the other. The fire fighter, fortunately, does not have to memorize these temperatures, but a general knowledge of them serves as a constant reminder that combustibles in the vicinity of a fire have, in comparison with the heat of the fire, relatively low "ignition temperatures" and that, as a consequence, there is an ever-present danger that fire will spread to them.

Fire point. The fire point is the lowest temperature at which a substance will give off vapors, which, when ignited, will continue to burn. The fire point is generally slightly above the flash point.

Flash point. The flash point is the lowest temperature at which a substance will give off enough vapors to form flammable mixtures of vapors and air (oxygen) immediately above its surface. The temperature at which this mixture will "flash" across the surface (but not burn), if a source of ignition is applied, is the flash point.

In the case of the flash point, the temperature is not high enough to increase the rate of "vaporization" to the point where it will generate a constant supply of fuel.

Vaporization. The rate of vaporization depends on the vapor pressure, which increases with the temperature. A flammable substance is, therefore, more hazardous at an elevated temperature than at normal temperature. It is pointed out that the solid or liquid substances do not burn; only the vapor which has combined with the oxygen in the air burns. The oxygen must be present to unite with the vapor in flame. Without oxygen the flame will smother.

The tendency of a liquid to vaporize is indicated by its flash point and fire point. The heat of a fire once started naturally increases the temperature of the liquid up to its boiling point. At this point the fire may no longer increase greatly in intensity because the heat supplied to the liquid by radiation from the fire approaches a maximum value, which is balanced by the heat used up in vaporizing or boiling the liquid. When a liquid is burning, its exposed surface is at, or above, the temperature corresponding to its fire point. If the burning liquid can be cooled below this temperature, the rate of vaporization will not provide sufficient fuel (vapor) to support continuous combustion.

Spontaneous ignition or combustion. When heat is generated by chemical action within a substance and the process continues to a point of ignition, the phenomenon is known as spontaneous ignition or spontaneous combustion. Usually, spontaneous heating begins with a slow oxidation which generates heat. As the heat increases the chemical action takes place at a progressively increasing rate until the "ignition temperature" is reached. Some substances reach the ignition temperature rapidly; other substances may take hours or days or even months; while other substances are not subject to spontaneous combustion. Substances subject to spontaneous combustion will differ in the degree of probability with which it will occur, but every such substance has a point in the scale of temperatures at which it will begin to burn. Oils that combine readily with the oxygen in the air are subject to spontaneous heating. When these oils (chiefly of animal or vegetable origin), are present in waste, rubbish, or other material, under conditions in which heat is produced faster than it is dissipated, the temperature rises and ignition may occur.

Explosive range. The temperature at which a flammable substance begins to burn is not necessarily the point at which it will explode. Although heat is a factor in causing explosions, the concentration of certain explosive gases in air within a container or enclosure is a determining cause of the explosion. In the case of gasoline, a vapor-air (oxygen) mixture containing more than 6 percent vapor is too "rich" to explode, and a mixture of less than 1.4 percent is too "lean" to explode. The range from 1.4 to 6 percent is the explosive range for gasoline. Concentrations below or above this range are said to be either "too lean" or "too rich" to explode. The concentration varies among explosive gases and it varies for the same gas under different conditions.

Classifying types of fires. Fire may be classified in four groups. These types are as follows:

Class A—Fires in ordinary combustible materials, such as mattresses, dunnage, piles of wood and shaving, canvas, etc. These fires are best extinguished by the quenching and cooling effects of quantities of water or water fog.

Class B—Fires in substances such as gasoline, oil, lubricating oil, diesel oil, tar, greases, etc. Here the blanketing or smothering effect of the extinguishing agent is of primary importance.

Class C—Fires in live electrical equipment, such as switchboard insulation, transformer terminals, etc. Here the extinguishing agents must be nonconducting so that electrical shock is not experienced by the fire fighter.

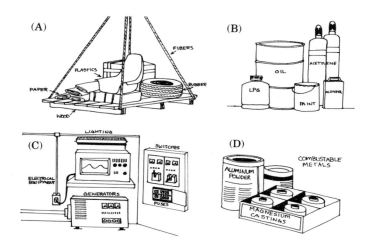

Fig. 30. Classes of fire.

Class D—Fires in combustible metals such as magnesium, sodium, titanium, lithium, etc.

Fighting a Fire

Fighting a fire is a subject that could fill several dozen volumes the size of this small book. Suffice it to say that the sailor's best approach to a fire on board his ship is to prevent it from happening in the first place. If this fails, then early discovery and quick and correct extinguishing is the best method of preserving his vessel.

Prevention. Prevention of fire is best accomplished by three actions. The first is to train the crew properly in the normal practice of good seamanship to avoid permitting the fire to take place. Examples of fire prevention behavior are:

1. Don't smoke in bed.
2. Don't throw cigarettes in wastebaskets.

3. Don't overload or jury-rig electrical circuits.
4. Do dispose of oily rags correctly.

The second important factor in preventing fire is proper maintenance. Frequent inspection of wiring and regular inspection and cleaning of galley exhaust vents is important. Smoke detection systems should be inspected and checked regularly.

The third and most important factor is proper training and planning for a fire. This may prevent a minor smoldering cord or small trash can fire from engulfing the entire ship.

Should a fire be discovered, see that it is reported to the proper authority at once. *After* the fire has been reported, take action to contain or control the fire until the ship's organization is brought into play.

It is important that crew members use common sense in the initial attack on a fire. If in an enclosed space, be sure you have a safe and unblockable means of escape and an alternate escape route. Be aware that smoke inhalation and reduced oxygen may cause loss of consciousness.

Finally, you must choose the correct extinguishing agent. If electricity is involved, soda acid or salt water must *never* be used. If it is a burning mattress or lumber, CO_2 is not very effective.

During preliminary attacks on fire, primary importance must be placed on individual safety. More detailed fire fighting techniques are available in other texts. Remember, you can never learn too much about fire. Your life and your ship's survival are on the line.

Portable fire extinguishers. The table below lists the types of portable extinguishers commonly used on merchant vessels, the type of fires for which they are suitable, the method of operation, and the maintenance required:

Foam

Use on: "A" and "B." Do not use on electrical fires.

How to operate: Turn upside down. Direct nozzle at base of fire. Recharge.

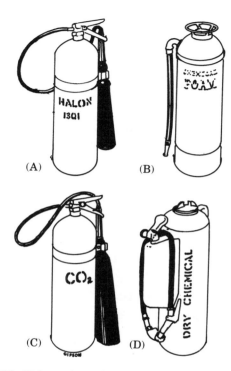

Fig. 31. (A) The Halon extinguisher. (B) A foam fire extinguisher. (C) A carbon dioxide extinguisher. (D) A dry chemical extinguisher.

Yearly maintenance: Discharge. Clean hose and inside of extinguisher thoroughly. Recharge as directed on nameplate.

Carbon Dioxide

Use on: "B" and "C." CO_2 extinguishers are not permitted in passenger or crew quarters.

How to operate: Open valve to release snow and gas. Direct discharge at flames in a slow sweeping motion.

Yearly maintenance: Weigh. Recharge if weight is 10 percent or more under required charge. Check hose and horn.

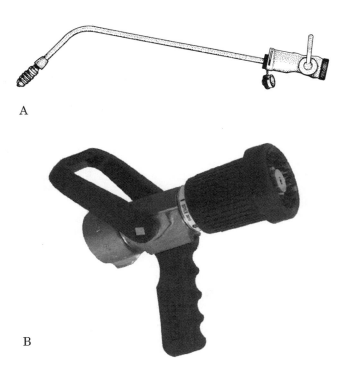

A

B

Fig. 32. (A) A fog nozzle applicator. The nozzle valve handle has 3 positions. In forward position, it is "off." In middle position (straight up and down) it is for fog. In back position, it is for solid stream. (B) A newer and more versatile nozzle, which is replacing the applicator shown in (A) both in the U.S. Merchant Marine and the U.S. Navy, is this pistol grip nozzle which permits varying the stream. Courtesy Akron Brass Co.

Dry Chemical

Use on: "B" and "C"

How to operate: Operate release and direct discharge at base of flames in sweeping motion.

Yearly maintenance: Examine pressure cartridge and replace if end is punctured or if the cartridge has leaked. See that dry chemical is not caked. In pressure type, see that pressure gauge is in operating range and that there is sufficient quantity of dry chemical.

Fire-fighting techniques. Fire in explosives and certain other dangerous substances, such as ammonium nitrate (NH_4NO_3), cannot always be put out by using CO_2 or steam. Many such substances can provide their own oxygen. These fires can often be fought with water. Powdered magnesium metal can burn in CO_2. Sodium metal will burn vigorously in water. When these types of cargo are carried, careful consideration should be given shipper's instructions, pertinent dangerous cargo regulations, and other responsible sources of information, so that proper action will be known in event of fire.

An efficient method of fighting oil fires is the use of water spray applied with a combination nozzle. Spray nozzles disperse the water in the form of fine droplets. This increases the speed with which the cooling capacity of the water becomes effective, reducing the amount of water required to cool a fire below the temperature at which burning will occur. In addition to putting out fires on the surface of liquids, an important use of fog may be the cooling of bulkheads of a compartment enclosing a fire. Fog also can be used as a shield behind which it is possible to advance in putting out a fire. Temperatures must be lowered beneath the point at which reignition will occur behind you as you advance using the fog nozzle. Care must be taken that sufficient oxygen is present to sustain life after a fire which used oxygen within a space. Fixed water spray systems are also used to protect pump rooms of tank vessels.

Foam is used for extinguishing flammable liquid fires in boiler and machinery spaces of vessels and also for the protection of pump rooms and cargo tank areas of tank vessels. Proportioning equipment mixes concentrated foam liquid with water from the fire pump making a solution which is piped to nozzles where air is mixed to make the foam. Foam forms a blanket of closely knit bubbles which float on the flammable liquids and smother the fire. An advantage is that the foam blanket remains intact, thus preventing reignition. For deck systems the foam is applied either by turret nozzles or by hand hose line nozzles. Fixed systems are installed in pump rooms and boiler and machinery spaces.

Safety Devices

Protection for breathing is furnished by two related but distinctly different types of equipment. These are the oxygen breathing apparatus and the gas mask, which is now properly called the "air mask respirator." The difference between the two is extremely important, and ignorance may cost you your life. Oxygen breathing apparatus provides an independent source of breathing air that is separate from the air that surrounds you. An air mask respirator simply uses the air that surrounds you. And if there is not enough oxygen in the surrounding air, you will become unconscious and die if you are not rescued.

Oxygen breathing apparatus. Breathing apparatus come in several difference configurations, but they all have one thing in common. They all provide an independent source of breathing air that is separate from the air that surrounds you. They can be either: 1) a hose line unit with full-face mask (where you are connected to distant air bottles or pumps via an umbilical air hose; 2) a self-contained breathing apparatus (SCBA) where you carry an air bottle on your back that supplies your face mask, or; 3) a pre-placed rescue air pack that consists of a small air bottle (5 minute) connected to a canvas or plastic hood that covers your entire head.

The most common type of breathing apparatus used aboard ships today is the self-contained breathing apparatus (see figure 33). This apparatus provides the wearer with an independent and portable supply of fresh clean air. It consists of a compressed air cylinder mounted into a harness that is worn over the shoulders and fitted with a waist belt. An air hose leads from the bottle valve to a regulator that adjusts air flow to a full-face mask. The regulator can be a positive-pressure or demand type. Regulators are also fitted with an emergency bypass that permits air to flow directly from the bottle to the face piece, in case a problem develops in the

Fig. 33. A self-contained breathing apparatus. This Scott Air Pak is one of several such devices approved by the Coast Guard. At left it is shown properly adjusted by the wearer. When not in use, it is stowed in a carrying case.

regulator. Keeping a positive-pressure (over-pressure) air flow in the face mask will help prevent the infiltration of smoke into a poorly adjusted mask; however, care must still be taken to properly tighten all of the straps for the face mask. Modern SCBA units are identical to those worn by many city fire departments. SCBAs have replaced older OBA (oxygen breathing apparatus) for a variety of reasons. OBAs were carried on ships for years because they chemically produced their own oxygen from canisters and thus could be used over and over by simply changing canisters. Now, many ships are fitted with their own air compressor that can refill standard SCBA compressed-air cylinders.

Air mask respirators. Most respirators can be fitted with different types of chemical cartridges for filtering different types of gases or vapors. Other filters, or sometimes pre-filters, are designed to remove only particulate matter from the air by means of a trapping fibrous material. Respirators can be either full-face masks or half-face masks and are tightened snugly about the face with a head strap arrangement. Many companies prohibit crewmen from wearing beards because of respirator wearing requirements. Obviously, the half-face masks do not cover the wearer's eyes and thus will not prevent gases from being absorbed through the eye membranes.

For proper use, the headbands of the mask are adjusted so that the face piece is held very tightly against the face in order to prevent the entrance of gases under the mask. If a respirator is worn incorrectly, it will do the wearer little good. In fact, it may provide the wearer with a false sense of protection and may lead to severe injury. Occupational regulations now require that workmen actually be "fitted" with the proper size of respirator to ensure a good face seal. When wearing a respirator, the wearer can test the tightness of his respirator by covering the filter intakes with his hands and breathing in. If the mask collapses initially and remains so, then the face piece is air tight.

As the respirator wearer inhales, air is brought through the intake canisters and passes through the filter element. Different filter elements are available to chemically filter out selected types of gases or vapors, so be sure to carefully check the type of filter element that your respirator is fitted with. These filter elements can be changed with different filter types to filter out other families of gas. The mask is fitted with a one-way exhaust valve to permit exhaled breath to exit the mask. Masks must be kept clean to ensure proper operation and are usually stored in their own plastic bag for protection and cleanliness. Cleaning is normally accomplished with warm water and mild soap. You can also use a low concentration of medical biocide soap to sanitize the mask.

Air respirators simply purify the air breathed through them and should not be used in an atmosphere containing less than 19% oxygen. If there is any doubt as to the oxygen content of a space or compartment, use an atmosphere tester before entering.

Combustible gas indicators. The presence of combustible gases aboard ship can be detected by a gas chemist or by a ship's officer trained to use a combustible gas indicator. There are several types of gas indicators on the market, and all are very similar. The Drager Detector is shown, and its use is described.

Fig. 34. A combustible gas indicator. The Drager Detector is shown. At the left is the case containing several tubes for sampling different types of gas. At right is the detector with the tube inserted.

The Drager Detector consists of a gas detector pump which is also called the bellows pump, and a glass detector tube which is different for each type of gas to be sampled. Both tips of the glass tube are broken off, and the tube is inserted into the bellows pump. By squeezing the pump a prescribed number of times, the gas which is to be sampled is drawn into the tube. The length of the discoloration of the chemical in the tube indicates the concentration of gas in percentage of volume. If the user has a complete set of detector tubes furnished by the manufacturer, he will be able to detect over 125 different toxic vapors and gases.

Safety line. Before entering a confined space, with either a work respirator or an emergency type of breathing apparatus, the wearer should be attached to a safety line or lifeline device. Some confined space entry procedures will require the worker to wear a special rescue extraction harness. This harness, connected by a small wire to a hand winch, will permit co-workers outside the space to winch out a person in trouble without having to actually enter the confined space themselves.

When using a traditional lifeline, somebody should tend the line to be alert for signals from the entrant. The standard line pull signals should be written on a metal plate on both ends of the line. The memory aid for these signals is **OATH:**

One pull—**O**k
Two pulls—**A**dvancing—give slack.
Three pulls—**T**ake in slack—I'm moving back.
Four pulls—**H**elp

3. First Aid
and Safe Practices Aboard Ship

First aid, in any situation, consists of the emergency treatment of the sick and/or injured until competent medical or surgical help can be obtained. At sea, however, you may well be the only medical help available.

There are some general rules to keep in mind in almost any emergency situation.

1. Keep the patient lying down until the extent of his injuries can be determined.
2. Check for breathing, bleeding, and signs of shock.
3. Remove only enough clothing to get a clear idea of the extent of the injury.
4. Reassure the casualty. Explain that you have help coming and that everything will be fine.
5. Avoid allowing the casualty to see his injury. Even a minor injury may appear severe to the injured person.
6. Never attempt to give an unconscious person anything by mouth, not even water.
7. Do not move the casualty until first aid measures are complete.
8. Always move a casualty feet first, except when going up a ladder.

Before discussing the care of different types of injuries, a few words about *you*. When an injury occurs, whether one or many, excitement and confusion arise. In these situations you will have to force yourself to *keep calm*. Never permit yourself to become overly excited and confused. Act quickly with efficiency and confidence. Doing this will reassure the casualty that everything that can be done is being done.

If there are many casualties, enlist the help of those individuals not seriously injured. This will keep them occupied and from feeling sorry for themselves.

Cardiopulmonary Resuscitation

CPR (cardiopulmonary resuscitation) is the root treatment for any illness or injury. If you spend time working on the injury itself, whether bleeding, fracture, wounds, etc., and the casualty is not breathing and his heart is not pumping blood through his veins, you may be patching up a dead person. In short, the first thing to be checked on any casualty is breathing and pulse. This is because if the brain, the computer that tells the rest of the body what and how to do it, is without oxygen for a period of 4 to 6 minutes, its cells start to die. These cells can never be regenerated. After about 10 minutes, it is possible that a significant number of brain cells have died so that even if "lucky" enough to get heart and breathing started, the casualty may already be a "vegetable." Therefore, if breathing and/or pulse are absent, CPR must be started immediately. The procedures for CPR are as follows:

1. Establish an airway. The tongue is the most frequent cause of an airway obstruction (figure 36). When a person is unconscious, the lower jaw relaxes and falls back. The tongue, being attached to the lower jaw, also falls back and blocks the passage of air to the lungs. With certain exceptions, the best way to correct this obstruction is to hyperextend the head, which will thrust the jaw forward, lifting the tongue from the back of the throat, allowing a free flow of air to and from the lungs. This may be all that is needed for the casualty to start breathing on his own. If breathing is in doubt, place your ear over the casualty's mouth so you may feel and/or hear any breathing. If there is no breathing, blow four (4) full deep breaths into the casualty's mouth (hold nose

closed), not allowing the lungs to deflate completely—
then check the carotid pulse.

2. Check to see if the casualty is still not breathing. Then
   start mouth-to-mouth artificial ventilation at the rate of
   one (1) breath every five (5) seconds or twelve (12) times
   per minute until spontaneous breathing starts.

3. Check carotid pulse to see if the heart is beating (see
   figure 37). The carotid arteries are on either side of the
   "Adam's apple." Place 2 fingers on the Adam's apple and
   slide them to the cleft on either side and press lightly to
   feel the pulse. If you do not feel a pulse, start artificial
   circulation by placing the heel of your hand on the lower
   half of the sternum (breastbone), not the xyphoid, which
   is the very tip of the sternum. Compress the chest 1½ to
   2 inches.

   Compress the chest at the rate of 80 to 100 times
   per minute. This is done by compressing the chest 15
   times, then giving 2 full ventilations (breaths) into the
   casualty until he becomes conscious or the heart starts
   beating on its own and spontaneous breathing returns.

The Coast Guard requires that all licensed officers be
certified in CPR. This must be renewed every two years, and
is particularly important because if there have been any
changes in the recommended procedures, the individual will
learn them when he updates his certificate. Although nonli-
censed personnel are not required to have CPR training, it
is strongly recommended that able seamen also receive certification. A shipmate's life may be saved.

Near Drowning

Drowning or near drowning is caused by asphyxiation due to
submersion. All near-drowning victims suffer from acute
asphyxia. There is a lowering of arterial oxygen (hypoxemia),
and an increase in the metabolic acidosis which persists in
those who have aspirated fluid.

It is useless to attempt to drain water from the lungs of
either a freshwater or a sea water near-drowning victim.

However, placing the patient in the Trendelenburg position (head and shoulders lower than the abdomen and pelvis), may promote drainage.

Often victims of submersion swallow water, which fills the stomach and prevents movement of the diaphragm. Roll the victim face down and lift him just anterior to the pelvis. Any water will drain out of his stomach by gravity.

Roll the victim over and begin the routine CPR as follows:

1. Establish an airway.
2. Check carotid pulse.
3. Start closed chest cardiac massage, alternating with positive pressure mouth-to-mouth ventilation.

	In Respiratory Arrest	*In Cardiac Arrest*
CAUSES	Airway obstruction Respiratory depression Cardiac arrest	Cardiac standstill Ventricular fibrillation Circulatory collapse
SYMPTOMS	Absence of respiration Cyanosis Dilated pupils	Absence of pulses Absence of respiration Dilated pupils
TREATMENT	Airway opened Breathing restored Circulation restored Definitive medical treatment sought	

Hypothermia

Survival in water has been a problem plaguing seamen for hundreds of years. In cold water this problem is increased because without heat the body functions soon deteriorate.

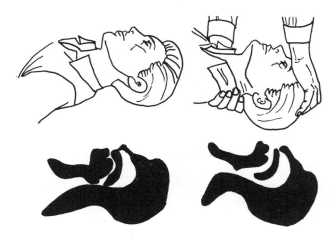

Fig. 36. The airway. The two sketches on the left show patient when assistance first arrives on scene. Lower jaw is relaxed, and passage of air to the lungs is blocked. Sketches on right show how airway is opened by hyperextending the head. This is the first step in the administration of CPR (cardiopulmonary resuscitation). CPR has taken the place of all older forms of reviving the unconscious or apparently drowned.

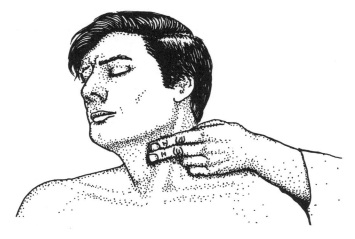

Fig. 37. The carotid pulse.

Numbness, loss of muscle control, and loss of consciousness are the symptoms of hypothermia.

The loss of body heat and subsequent reduction of body temperature can occur either in cold water or when exposed to cold air. If survival ashore in a cold atmosphere is going to be necessary for any length of time, the seaman should particularly avoid getting wet if at all possible. Layers of heavy clothing help insulate the body and prevent loss of heat.

Water is of much higher density than air and thus conducts heat away from the body much more rapidly than is the case with air. If clothing is porous, it does little to reduce the flow of heat. Nonporous clothing such as foul-weather gear or an exposure suit are preferred if exposure to cold is expected. The body should be kept in a tightly coiled position when in cold water to reduce surface contact and thus heat loss. Attempts to swim generally only compound the heat loss problem. Contrary to general belief, alcohol *increases* the rate of body heat loss.

The seaman should remember the following if he expects to survive in cold water:

1. Wear nonporous clothing if available. Foul-weather gear helps, but is not a replacement for an immersion suit.
2. Stay in water no longer than absolutely necessary.
3. Keep calm and keep body tightly coiled to reduce body heat loss (knees tucked up to chin).
4. Wear a life jacket.

The treatment for hypothermia victims is as follows:

1. Remove wet clothing.
2. Cover with warm blankets or have another person keep the victim warm by lying on top of or beside him.
3. Give stimulating drinks such as hot coffee or tea. Do not give alcohol.
4. Get the victim to a proper medical facility as soon as possible.
5. Handle the victim gently and with extreme care. His flesh may damage easily.

Management of Wounds and Injuries

By definition, a wound is a break in the continuity of body tissues involving an opening in the skin, and an injury is the disruption in the continuity of body tissues not necessarily involving the skin. With this in mind, you can see that all wounds may be classified as injuries, but not all injuries may be classified as wounds.

In wound prophylaxis keeping the break clean is of utmost importance. This can be accomplished by doing the following:

1. Make sure your hands are clean. Scrub them thoroughly with soap and hot water.
2. Place a piece of sterile bandage over the wound while cleaning the surrounding area.
3. If the wound is in a hairy area, shave the hair off 2 to 3 inches around the wound. (Never shave off any part of the eyebrow, as it may not grow back.)
4. If possible, flush the wound thoroughly with sterile saline solution. This will wash out any loose debris.
5. Apply a dry sterile dressing, using only sufficient pressure to stop bleeding.
6. If the casualty has not had a tetanus booster within the past six months, give 0.5 cc. of tetanus toxoid, injected into the arm to prevent "lock-jaw."
7. Start antibiotic therapy as indicated.

Control of Hemorrhage

Hemorrhage, or bleeding, is the escape of blood from arteries, veins, and capillaries because of a break in their walls. Control of active bleeding is urgent.

While external bleeding is very apparent, internal bleeding can be just as serious. The following symptoms will usually be present in both types of hemorrhage, but perhaps disregarded in external bleeding:

1. Pale skin or pale mucous membranes.
2. Subnormal temperature.

3. Increased pulse rate or possibly feeble and easily compressed or lost.
4. Blood pressure lowered.
5. Dilated pupils, slow in reacting to light.
6. Ringing in ears.
7. Faintness or fainting (may be first symptom).
8. Thirst due to dehydration.
9. Air hunger (yawning).
10. Impaired vision.

The treatment of internal hemorrhage can be accomplished only by surgery. Until a patient reaches a hospital, he must be kept alive with the aid of I.V.s (blood volume expanders), that can be used until whole blood is available at the hospital. Blood loss can produce hemorrhagic shock.

For external hemorrhage the steps for control are:

1. Local pressure by use of pressure dressings.
2. The use of a tourniquet, a constricting bond that can be placed around an extremity and tightened until the escaping blood flow stops. It should be used only as a last resort.

Management of Shock

Shock is a state of circulatory deficiency associated with depression of the vital processes of the body. The symptoms of shock are the following:

1. Eyes are glassy, lackluster; pupils are dilated; patient shows fear and/or apprehension.
2. Breathing is shallow and irregular.
3. Lips may be pale or cyanotic (bluish grey).
4. Skin is pale, cool, and moist or waxy.

The treatment for shock patients includes the following:

1. Keep patient lying on his back.
2. Raise feet 10 to 12 inches higher than head.

3. Keep patient warm by removing wet clothing and by covering with a blanket.
4. Ascertain cause and contact a physician.

Management of Burns

Burns are classified in several ways: by the extent of body surface burned, by the depth of the burn, and by the causative agent. Of these, extent of body surface burned plays the greatest role in survival. This is calculated by what is called the "Rule of Nines" (figure 38).

Using this as a basis, an adult having 15 percent of body surface burned, or a small child having 10 percent of body surface burned, can go into shock. If more than 20 percent of body surface is burned, it can endanger life. If 30 percent or more of body surface is burned, it is usually fatal.

Keeping the above in mind and adding another factor or classification of depth or degree will intensify the mortality rate of burn injuries.

First-degree burns involve only the outer layer of skin or epidermis. Mild sunburn is a good example.

Second-degree burns extend through the epidermis and involve the inner layers of skin or dermis, but not enough to prevent rapid regeneration of the skin. They are characterized by blisters and moderately severe pain.

Third-degree burns destroy both the epidermis and dermis along with underlying tissues. Severe pain may be absent because nerve endings have been destroyed. The color may range from white and lifeless, as in scalds, to black and charred, as in thermal or gas explosions. Skin grafts are generally required before complete healing can take place.

If the burn involves 20 percent or less of body surface burned, immerse the part in ice water. Where immersion is impractical, repeated applications of ice-cold moist towels to the burned area are advisable. Continue this ice-water treatment until no pain is felt. This could take anywhere from 30 minutes to 5 hours.

Treatment for pain of a first-degree burn should require no more than 1 or 2 aspirins for relief of discomfort; for

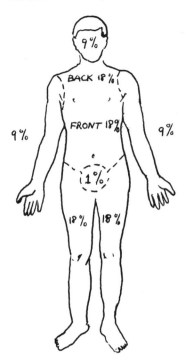

Fig. 38. "Rule of Nines" for analysis of burn treatment. Head = 9%, front of body = 18%, genital area = 1%, each leg = 18%.

moderately severe pain, as with second-degree burns, co-deine ½ grain (32 mg.) orally or by injection; for pain from extensive burns (third-degree), 8 to 20 mg. of morphine injected subcutaneously. Morphine should not be injected intramuscularly because of the probability of reduced peripheral circulation and possible morphine poisoning.

In burns as with other things that happen to, and within, the body, the body's own mechanisms take over and try to help right the wrong. In the case of burns, the body rushes fluid in the form of plasma to the site of the burn to help cool it. This causes a loss of fluid in other important parts of the body, including the blood stream. With a decrease in blood volume, shock is imminent. Therefore, these fluids must be replaced. If the casualty is conscious, he may be given liquids (coffee, tea, water, etc.) with salt added (about $1/4$ teaspoon to 8 ounces). If unconscious, an I.V. of sterile normal saline should be started (8 to 10 drops per minute).

Safe Practices

Observing the following practices will help avoid accidents and injuries aboard merchant ships.

Work clothes should fit well and be in good repair. Any loose dangling parts can catch on machinery or fittings. Pants cuffs should not be used on trousers. Safety shoes can prevent injury to toes from falling objects. Composition traction soles help prevent slips and falls on wet or oily decks. Gloves with gauntlets can easily get caught when handling lines on a warping head.

Goggles should be worn anytime there is danger of injury to the eyes. Activities potentially dangerous include chipping paint or rust, sharpening tools on a power wheel, or letting go the anchor.

Only safety shackles with locknuts and cotter pins should be used aloft. Shackles used elsewhere should be wired whenever there is danger that the pin may tend to back out.

Bridles or slings for pontoons or hatch beams should have lanyards secured at each end above hooks so that there is no need to endanger hands or fingers. When using hydraulic or mechanical hatch openings, be sure safety hooks are locked and pinned. When opening or closing hatches, be sure all hands stand well clear.

Don't stand in the bight of a line.

Whether on deck or dockside, be alert for cargo operations. Do not walk near cargo operations until the longshore signalman indicates that it is safe to do so.

Don't leave manholes, floor plates, or hatches open without stanchions and guard ropes in place. Use lights and a warning sign to keep the unwary from straying into danger.

Don't cover open or partly open hatches with tarpaulins.

Use a hardhat when working cargo or when a member of a lifeboat crew.

When only one section of hatch is being worked, hatch beams or pontoons that can be hit by drafts of cargo or caught by hooks should be secured by locking devices or lashed in position. No one should stand on a section of an open hatch during cargo operations.

Compartments which have been closed for a long time, especially tanks or double bottoms, should be checked and found "gas free" and with sufficient oxygen before anyone is allowed to enter.

Cleaning compounds must be used with care and instructions read to be sure that injury to eyes or skin will not occur. Such substances as lye, boiler compounds, oxalic acid, caustic soda, etc., should be used with care. Some detergents can cause rapid rotting of ropes used for bos'n's chairs or stages.

Before men go aloft or over the side, gantlines, blocks, stages, etc., should be tested. Tests are simple and need little time.

Make sure the electricity is turned off before working on a constant tension winch. Should your clothes get caught between the warping head and the mooring line, you may be seriously injured or killed.

Compartments being painted should be well ventilated. Men using spray painting gear should have respiratory protection, face masks, filters, etc.

Never smoke while lying down in your bunk. Don't smoke near open hatches. Don't toss cigarettes or ashes out of portholes. They can blow back aboard, down ventilators, or burn through tarpaulins and start fires in a hold.

Secure pilot ladders to padeyes on deck, not to chain or pipe rails. Ladders must be checked to see that all slack is out by putting weight on them while keeping a firm grip before the pilot comes aboard or departs the ship.

Before going up the stack near a whistle, ask permission from the mate on watch.

Before going up the masts near the radio antennae, get permission from the mate on watch and inform the radio officer. Avoid standing close to a radio or radar antenna in operation.

Aloft, over the side, or going up or down ladders, remember: "One hand for the ship, one for yourself."

Remember that the wise seaman always wears a belt with his dungarees or other work pants. Otherwise, his shipmate who reaches to grab him when he slips and starts to go over the side may wind up holding only an empty pair of pants.

Use a flashlight in dark areas. Do not use a match. Always walk with a flashlight in dimly lit areas. Don't show lights in a way that will blind the lookout on the bow or the mate on the bridge.

Stepladders or straight ladders used aboard ship should be lashed in place. Lanyards fitted near the upper end are useful for this purpose. The use of hooks on ladders has caused many accidents.

Insure that electric tools are grounded before use.

Lift with legs and thigh muscles. Do not lift with your back.

Remember that oily decks cause slips. This is a frequent cause of injury.

Help protect beaches and wildlife—don't dump or throw overboard oil or oily waste. Don't dump garbage near the coastline.

Do not overstress any line, particularly synthetic line. If a synthetic line parts, it lashes out with the greatest force.

The windlass should not be left in gear. Do not take it out of gear until the brake is secure.

Always return a fire extinguisher to its proper location.

Do not leave a fire extinguisher in an empty condition. Turn it in to the bos'n or chief mate.

Never use defective electrical equipment.

Do not use fire hoses for any purpose other than fire fighting or fire drills.

Do not handle wire without gloves. Work gloves should be loose fitting and easily removed.

Do not make stage lines or manropes fast to a pipe rail or removable section of rail.

When handling a rope or wire on a warping head, make sure someone is at the controls of the winch.

Be very careful surging synthetic rope on a bitt because it can fuse. It is much better practice to slack back on the winch.

Insure that snatch blocks and shackles are stronger than the rope or wire with which they will be used.

When handling blocks under strain, keep fingers out of the way of falls, sheaves, and hooks. This is particularly important when hooking on a lifeboat.

Use a marlinespike to help lining up bolt holes.

Never leave a load suspended from a boom head.

Use the proper clamps to secure a fall to a winch drum.

Haul a man aloft by hand, not by winch.

Make sure that all tools taken aloft have lanyards. They should be carried in a bucket.

Use a line to lower a light into a hold or tank. Do not lower it by its own cable.

If you are going to leave a cluster light in a cargo hold, insure that it is disconnected.

4. The Able Seaman

The following information concerning requirements and certification as an able seaman is reproduced from the *Code of Federal Regulations: Title 46—Shipping*, Subparts 12.05 and 12.07 (Washington, D.C.: U.S. Government Printing Office, 1982).

Subpart 12.05—Able Seaman

§ 12.05-1 Certification required.

(a) Every person employed in a rating as able seaman on any United States vessel requiring certificated able seamen, before signing articles of agreement, shall present to the master, his or her certificate as able seaman (issued in the form of a merchant mariner's document).

(b) No certificate as able seaman is required of any person employed on any tug or towboat on the bays and sounds connected directly with the seas, or on any unrigged vessel except seagoing barges or tank barges.

(c) The following categories of able seaman are established:

(1) Able Seaman—Any Waters, Unlimited.

(2) Able Seaman—Limited.

(3) Able Seaman—Special.

(4) Able Seaman—Special (OSV).

[CGD 80-131, 45 FR 69240, Oct. 20, 1980]

§ 12.05-3 General requirements.

To qualify for certification as able seaman an applicant must:

(a) Be at least 18 years of age;

(b) Pass the prescribed physical examination;

(c) Meet the sea service or training requirements set forth in this part;

(d) Pass an examination demonstrating ability as an able seaman and lifeboatman; and,

(e) Speak and understand the English language as would be required in performing the general duties of able seaman and during an emergency aboard ship.

[CGD 80-131, 45 FR 69240, Oct. 20, 1980]

§ 12.05-5 Physical requirements.

(a) All applicants for a certificate of service as able seaman shall be required to pass a physical examination given by a medical officer of the United States Public Health Service and present to the Officer in Charge, Marine Inspection, a certificate executed by the Public Health Service Officer. Such certificate shall attest to the applicant's acuity of vision, color sense, hearing, and general physical condition. In exceptional cases where an applicant would be put to great inconvenience or expense to appear before a medical officer of the United States Public Health Service, the physical examination and certification may be made by any other reputable physician.

(b) The medical examination for an able seaman is the same as for an original license as a deck officer as set forth in § 10.02-5 of this subchapter. If the applicant is in possession of an unexpired deck license, the Officer in Charge, Marine Inspection, may waive the requirement for a physical examination.

§ 12.05-7 Service or training requirements.

(a) The minimum service required to qualify an applicant for the various categories of able seaman is as listed in this paragraph.

(1) Able Seaman—Any Waters, Unlimited. Three years service on deck on vessels operating on the oceans or the Great Lakes.

(2) Able Seaman—Limited. Eighteen months service on deck in vessels of 100 gross tons or over which operate in a

service not exclusively confined to the rivers and smaller inland lakes of the United States.

(3) Able Seaman—Special. Twelve months service on deck on vessels operating on the oceans, or the navigable water of the United States including the Great Lakes.

(4) Able Seaman—Special (OSV). Six months service on deck on vessels operating on the oceans, or the navigable waters of the United States including the Great Lakes.

NOTE: Employment considerations for the various categories of able seaman are contained in § 157.20-15 of this chapter.

(b) Training programs approved by the Commandant may be substituted for the required periods of service on deck as follows:

(1) A graduate of a school ship may be rated as able seaman upon satisfactory completion of the course of instruction. For this purpose, "school ship" is interpreted to mean an institution which offers a complete course of instruction, including a period of at sea training, in the skills appropriate to the rating of able seaman.

(2) Training programs, other than those classified as a school ship, may be substituted for up to one third of the required service on deck. The service/training ratio for each program is determined by the Commandant, who may allow a maximum of three days on deck service credit for each day of instruction.

(c) A certificate of service as "Able Seaman, Great Lakes—18 months' service," is considered equivalent to a certificate of service as "Able Seaman—Limited."

(d) A certificate of service as Able Seaman with the following route, vessel, or time restrictions is considered equivalent to a certificate of service as "Able Seaman—Special":

(1) "Any waters—12 months."

(2) "Tugs and towboats—any waters."

(3) "Bays and sounds—12 months, vessels 500 gross tons or under not carrying passengers."

(4) "Seagoing barges—12 months."

(e) An individual holding a certificate of service endorsed as noted in paragraphs (c) or (d) of this section may have his

or her merchant mariner's document endorsed with the equivalent category, upon request.
[CGD 80-131, 45 FR 69240, Oct. 20, 1980]

§ 12.05-9 Examination and demonstration of ability.

(a) Before an applicant is certified as able seaman, he shall prove to the satisfaction of the Coast Guard by oral or written examination and by actual demonstration, his knowledge of seamanship and his ability to carry out effectively all the duties that may be required of an able seaman, including those of a lifeboatman. He shall demonstrate that:

(1) He has been trained in all the operations connected with the launching of lifeboats and liferafts and the use of oars and sail;

(2) He is acquainted with the practical handling of the boats themselves; and

(3) He is capable of taking command of a boat's crew.

(b) The oral or written examination shall be conducted only in the English language and shall consist of questions regarding:

(1) Lifeboats and liferafts, the names of their essential parts, and a description of the required equipment;

(2) The clearing away, swinging out, and lowering of lifeboats and liferafts, and handling of lifeboats under oars and sails, including questions relative to the proper handling of a boat in a heavy sea;

(3) The operation and functions of commonly used types of davits;

(4) The applicant's knowledge of nautical terms; boxing the compass, either by degrees or points according to his experience; running lights, passing signals, and fog signals for vessels on the high seas, in inland waters, or on the Great Lakes depending upon the waters on which the applicant has had service; and distress signals; and,

(5) The applicant's knowledge of commands in handling the wheel by obeying orders passed to him as "wheelsman," and knowledge of the use of engineroom telegraph or bellpull signals.

(c) In the actual demonstration, the applicant shall show his ability by taking command of a boat and directing the operation of clearing away, swinging out, lowering the boat into the water, and acting as coxswain in charge of the boat under oars. He shall demonstrate his ability to row by actually pulling an oar in the boat. He shall also demonstrate knowledge of the principal knots, bends, splices, and hitches in common use by actually making them.

(c-1) The applicant must demonstrate to the satisfaction of the Officer in Charge, Marine Inspection, his knowledge of pollution laws and regulations, procedures for discharge containment and cleanup, and methods for disposal of sludge and waste material from cargo and fueling operations.

(d) Any person who is in valid possession of a certificate as able seaman endorsed, "any waters—12 months," and who can produce documentary evidence of sufficient service to qualify for a certificate as able seaman endorsed, "any waters—unlimited," may be issued a new document bearing this endorsement without additional professional examination. The applicant shall surrender for cancellation the document bearing the limited endorsement. No physical examination will be required at the time of this exchange unless it is found that the applicant obviously suffers from some physical or mental infirmity to a degree that in the opinion of the Officer in Charge, Marine Inspection, would render him incompetent to perform the usual duties of an able seaman at sea. If such condition is believed to exist, the applicant shall be required to undergo an examination by a medical officer of the Public Health Service to determine his competency.

(83 Stat. 852 (42 U.S.C. 4321, et. seq.))

[CGFR 65-50, 30 FR 16640, Dec. 30, 1965, as amended by CGD 71-161R, 37 FR 28263, Dec. 21, 1972]

§ 12.05-11 General provisions respecting merchant mariner's documents endorsed as able seaman.

(a) The holder of a merchant mariner's document endorsed for the rating of able seaman may serve in any unlicensed rating in the deck department without obtaining an additional endorsement.

(b) A merchant mariner's document endorsed as able seaman will also be considered a certificate of efficiency as lifeboatman without further endorsement.

(c) This type of document will describe clearly the type of able seaman certificate which it represents, e.g.: able seaman—any waters; able seaman—any waters, 12 months; able seaman—Great Lakes, 18 months; able seaman—on freight vessels, 500 gross tons or less on bays or sounds, and on tugs, towboats, and barges on any water.

Subpart 12.07—General Requirements for Issuance of Temporary Certificates of Service for Able Seamen on Offshore Supply Vessels

AUTHORITY: Pub L. 96-378; (46 U.S.C. 223, 224, 390-390g, 404, 404-1, 672, 673; 49 U.S.C. 1655(b)); 49 CFR 1.46 (b))

SOURCE: CGD 80-131, 45 FR 69240, Oct. 20, 1980, unless otherwise noted.

§ 12.07-1 Eligibility.

A person is eligible for a temporary certificate of service as Able Seaman—Special (OSV), for offshore supply vessels if:

(a) Application is made on or before January 6, 1981; and,

(b) The applicant was serving in an equivalent capacity on board an offshore supply vessel as defined by 46 U.S.C. 404-1, on or before January 1, 1979.

§ 12.07-5 Application procedure.

(a) A person may apply for a temporary certificate of service as Able Seaman—Special (OSV), at any Coast Guard Marine Inspection or Marine Safety Office.

(b) Application shall be made upon Coast Guard Form "Application for Temporary License or Certificate of Service for Crews of Offshore Supply Vessels."

§ 12.07-7 Service under an acknowledgment of application.

(a) Upon receipt of the completed application, the Officer in Charge, Marine Inspection, issues an "acknowledgment of application" to the applicant. Upon receipt of this acknowledgment, the applicant is deemed to be in compliance with the statutes dealing with certification of merchant marine personnel pending issuance of a temporary certificate or expiration of the acknowledgment of application.

(b) An acknowledgment of application is subject to suspension and revocation on the same grounds and procedures as provided by 46 U.S.C. 239.

(c) An acknowledgment of application shall remain valid until October 7, 1982.

§ 12.07-10 Issuance of temporary certificates of service.

(a) An Officer In Charge, Marine Inspection, may issue temporary certificates of service on or before October 6, 1982, to persons who have applied under § 12.07-5 and meet the requirements of § 12.07-15.

(b) Temporary certificates of service issued under the provisions of this part:

(1) Authorize service only upon offshore supply vessels;

(2) Remain valid for a period of three years from the date of issuance;

(3) May not be raised in grade;

(4) Are not renewable except for replacement occasioned by loss; and,

(5) Are subject to suspension and revocation on the same grounds and procedures as provided by 46 U.S.C. 239.

(c) Authority to issue temporary certificates of service of Able Seaman—Special (OSV), expires on October 7, 1982.

§ 12.07-15 Requirements for temporary certificates of service.

(a) An applicant for a temporary certificate of service as Able Seaman—Special (OSV), must meet the:

(1) Age requirements of § 12.05-3;

(2) Physical requirements of § 12.05-5; and,

(3) The citizenship requirements of § 12.02-13 and §12.02-14 before such certificate of service shall be issued.

(b) An applicant for a temporary certificate of service shall present to the Officer in Charge, Marine Inspection, letters, discharges, or other official documents certifying the amount and character of sea service, and the names of the vessels on which acquired. The Officer in Charge, Marine Inspection, must be satisfied as to the bona fides of all evidence of sea service or training presented and may reject any evidence not considered to be authentic or which does not sufficiently outline the amount, type and character of service.

(c) The minimum service required to obtain a temporary certificate of service as Able Seaman—Special (OSV) is 95 days service as master, mate or able seaman on board off-shore supply vessels.

NOTE: A twelve hour work day is equivalent to one day of the above service requirements. An eight hour work day is equivalent to two thirds of a service day.

(d) Service as master, mate or able seaman on board offshore supply vessels while holding the acknowledgment of application issued in accordance with §12.07-7 may be utilized to meet the sea service requirements of paragraph (c) of this section.

§ 12.07-20 Possession of temporary certificate of service or acknowledgment of application.

An individual employed in a certificated capacity upon an offshore supply vessel under a valid temporary certificate or acknowledgment of application must have the document in his or her possession and available for examination at all times.

Topics to Be Mastered

There are many books which will help seamen to improve their knowledge of their job. While some tasks can be easily made clear by practical experience, a combination of study and on-the-job work is the best way of becoming skilled. The following information does not try to cover the whole field, but sets forth some of the things sailors have to know to do their work safely and efficiently.

Anchor and Anchor Chain

Practically all ships of any size use the patent or stockless anchor, which is shown in figure 39. Although the old-fashioned or admiralty anchor is still unmatched in holding power ton for ton, it is rarely seen today because it is clumsy and awkward to use. A ship's anchor will weigh roughly 1 to 1½ pounds for each ton of a vessel's displacement. An anchor works like a pick axe. When driven into the ground, the pick will require a tremendous amount of force to pull it loose with a straight pull on the handle. By lifting the handle, however, a leverage is obtained which breaks it free. An anchor holds because a long cable causes the pull on the anchor to be in line with the shank. To break the anchor free, the cable is taken in. This lifts the shank of the anchor, producing a leverage which loosens its hold.

The large, heavy chains which hold the anchors are called anchor cables. The length of a ship's cable is standardized by the American Bureau of Shipping and is based on length, breadth, tonnage, and freeboard of the vessel. The chain is

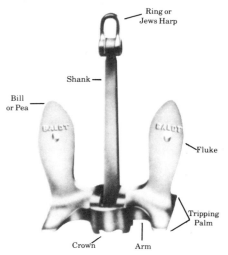

Fig. 39. A Baldt stockless anchor. Courtesy Baldt, Inc.

divided into "shots," which are connected by detachable links and are 15 fathoms in length. Since a fathom is 6 feet in length, a shot is equal to 90 feet.

The anchor cable is marked both by paint and turns of wire at each shot as follows:

1 shot—1 turn of wire on first stud from each side of the detachable link and white paint on the stud link on either side of the detachable link.

2 shots—2 turns of wire on the second stud from each side of the detachable link and white paint on the 2 stud links on either side of the detachable link.

3 shots—3 turns of wire on the third stud from each side of the detachable link and white paint on the 3 stud links on either side of the detachable link.

For each additional shot one more turn of wire is added and one more stud link on either side of the detachable link is added.

Compasses

There are two basic types of compasses. Most commercial vessels have a gyrocompass, and lifeboats are required to have a magnetic compass. The gyrocompass indicates true north and derives its directive force from the rotation of a motor-driven gyroscope. The magnetic compass derives its directive force from the earth's natural magnetic field.

Gyrocompass. As a mechanical-electrical device which requires ship's power to function, the gyrocompass only needs minor correction and points very close to true north. However, it is subject to mechanical breakdown, precession, high latitude errors, and improper speed and latitude settings. These errors can be significant. The gyrocompass must be checked frequently by azimuths and by comparison with the magnetic compass.

The magnetic compass. The standard compass on a ship is a magnetic compass and it serves as a backup for the gyrocompass. (The standard compass course is usually abbreviated "psc," per standard compass.) It is located as

Fig. 40. U.S. Navy 7½-inch compass. Courtesy Defense Mapping Agency Hydrographic Center.

high as possible in the ship to eliminate as much of the ship's magnetic field upon it as possible. Magnetic compasses must be corrected to eliminate error called deviation caused by the steel in the structure of the ship or boat. After this error is compensated for, or corrected, the magnetic compass points approximately to magnetic north. This differs from true north by variation, which is the difference between magnetic north and true north. Variation is different in all locations and is generally given on the navigational chart.

Compass courses. Compass courses on merchant ships are given in degrees. Boxing the compass helps give a sense of direction. The following table gives the direction by degrees as well as by points. There are 32 points, of which four (N, S, E, and W) are cardinal and four (NE, SE, SW, and NW) are intercardinal. Each point equals 11¼ degrees. Quarter points (for example N¼ E) are rarely, if ever, used today.

Name	Points	Degrees
North	0	0° 0'0"
N by E	1	11° 15'
NNE	2	22° 30'
NE by N	3	33° 45'
NE	4	45° 00'
NE by E	5	56° 15'

ENE	6	67° 30′
E by N	7	78° 45′
East	8	90° 00′
E by S	9	101° 15′
ESE	10	112° 30′
SE by E	11	123° 45′
SE	12	135° 00′
SE by S	13	146° 15′
SSE	14	157° 30′
S by E	15	168° 45′
South	16	180° 00′
S by W	17	191° 15′
SSW	18	202° 30′
SW by S	19	213° 45′
SW	20	225° 00′
SW by W	21	236° 15′
WSW	22	247° 30′
W by S	23	258° 45′
West	24	270° 00′
W by N	25	281° 15′
WNW	26	292° 30′
NW by W	27	303° 45′
NW	28	315° 00′
NW by N	29	326° 15′
NNW	30	337° 30′
N by W	31	348° 45′
North	32	360° 00′

Buoyage

The able seaman should have a rudimentary knowledge of the buoyage system used in the United States. Further information can be found in Bowditch or *Dutton's* (see References, p. 167). The following, however, is basic:

When entering a channel from the sea, red nun buoys will be on the starboard side, green can buoys will be on the port side. If lighted buoys are used, lights on starboard side will be red, lights on port side will be green.

When entering a channel from the sea, numbers increase numerically as land is approached (2, 4, 6, etc.). Red buoys have even numbers, green buoys have odd numbers.

Midchannel buoys are vertically striped red and white. If lighted, the light will be white.

Steering

The first thing you must know when learning to steer is that the ship's head, indicated by the lubber line, moves, while the compass *always* points to north. The job is to bring the lubber line back to the degree marking that is the desired course. It may help to remember: "Come right to add. Come left to subtract." For example, if steering course 250° and ordered to come to course 270°, apply right rudder or add 20°. "Right rudder" means turn the wheel to the right or clockwise. "Left rudder" means turn the wheel left or counterclockwise.

When at the helm do not keep a knife or wrench in your pocket because the iron in them will cause an error in the magnetic compass.

When steering in rough weather, the ship may yaw and roll without getting seriously off course. The halfway point between the compass headings at the ends of the roll or yaw is the course being steered.

A skilled helmsman—or wheelsman—steers with the least possible amount of rudder to maintain the course. Too much rudder cuts down the speed and wastes fuel. Whether steering or standing by on the bridge when the automatic pilot or "Iron Mike" is being used, the helmsman should help the watch officer to see that the ship is on course and that the rudder is being used properly. Remember that if on the Iron Mike, the proper "rudder" and "weather" adjustments must be used. Remember also that if the wheel is turned, a change in course, not an immediate rudder command, results. A contributing factor to the *Torrey Canyon* disaster may have been that those in authority on the bridge forgot that the ship was on Iron Mike. In the confusion of the emergency, when the helmsman spun the wheel to make a radical course change, he was only changing course a small amount for each revolution of the wheel. He was not placing the rudder hard left or hard right.

A wheelsman should check the gyro steering repeater against the magnetic steering compass at least once every fifteen minutes. The gyro, being mechanical, can go wrong, and this simple check will show up errors. Together with the watch officer, the wheelsman should check the steering compass against the standard magnetic compass at least each hour and after a course change. Repeaters and the master gyro should also be checked at regular intervals. When the wheel is relieved, it is customary to tell the officer on watch the course being steered before leaving the bridge. This practice serves to help avoid errors.

When steering by landmarks, it is best to use those far away. Closer landmarks open rapidly on the bow as the ship gets near. When steering at night by stars, remember the stars change in direction as they move across the sky; so refer to the compass every few minutes.

Commands to the helmsman. A good helmsman learns the steering commands so well that they become second nature to him. A few of the more basic commands are given below:

Right (left) 5°, 10°, 15°, etc., rudder—Turn the wheel to the right (left) until the rudder is placed at the number of degrees ordered. This command is frequently used in making a change of course. The helmsman would then be ordered to steer the new course by such a command as "Steady on course_____°" in time to permit him to "meet her" on the new course. The complete command would be: "Right 10° rudder, steady on course 275°."

Give her more rudder—Increase the rudder angle. The command is given with the rudder already over when it is desired to make the ship turn more rapidly. The command should be followed by the exact number of degrees desired for the turn.

Meet her—Use rudder as necessary to check the swing. This command is given when the ship is nearing the desired course.

Ease the rudder to 15°, 10°, 5°, etc.—Decrease the rudder angle. The command is given when the ship is nearing its new heading, and it is desired to slow the swing.

Steady, steady as you go—Steer the course that the ship is heading when you receive the command. This command is given when, in changing course, the new course is reached or the ship is heading as desired.

Rudder amidships—Place the rudder amidships. The command may be given when the ship is turning, and it is desired to make her swing less rapidly.

Shift your rudder—Change from right to left rudder (or vice versa), an equal amount.

Mind your rudder—A warning that the ship is swinging to the right (left) of the ordered course because of bad steering. Pay attention!

Nothing to the right (left)—Do not let the ship's head move to the right (left) of the ordered course. This command is frequently used in a narrow channel.

How does she head?—A question to the helmsman. He should give the ship's head at the time. "200°, sir."

Keep her so—A command to the helmsman when he reports the ship's heading, and it is desired that he steady the ship down on that heading.

Very well—An acknowledgment from the master or conning officer after the helmsman has reported that an order has been carried out. It is never used by the helmsman. "Very well" is used rather than "all right," which might be confused with a command to use right rudder.

Come right (left) to course 120° [or whatever]—Put the rudder over right (left) and steady on course ordered.

Lookout. One of the most important jobs required of a seaman is standing lookout watch. When an object is reported, the bearing should be given accurately so that the captain or mate on watch can look in the right direction and see it. Since there is rarely a compass available to the lookout, he will make his report using relative bearings as shown in figure 41. It is important that the lookout line himself up with the ship's centerline so that he will make an accurate report. If it is daytime, it is helpful if he points.

On some vessels the lookout strikes bells on the half hour to indicate the passage of time, although this custom has fallen into disuse. During darkness the lookout checks the navigation lights every half hour and reports whether they are burning brightly or not.

If there is no telephone at the bow station, it is customary to indicate objects sighted on the starboard side with one stroke of the bell, objects sighted on the port side with two strokes, and objects dead ahead with three strokes.

An attentive lookout on the bow can often see objects in the water not easily seen by the officer on the bridge. Although the watch officer will scan the horizon frequently, he does have other duties. Therefore, the lookout should report everything he sees. This includes other vessels, navigational aids, discolored water, objects in the water, or anything unusual. It is better to report too much than too little. A lookout cannot allow his attention to be distracted. He cannot be assigned any other jobs. The safety of the ship is in his hands.

Lead Line

Merchant ships are equipped with fathometers or Doppler speed logs which register the depth of water, but seamen still have occasional use for the lead line and must be familiar with its use. The hand lead weighs about 7 to 14 pounds and is marked as indicated in figure 42.

The lead has its bottom hollowed out so that tallow or soap can be put in it to bring back a sample of the bottom. This process is called "arming the lead." If a ship or boat is going ahead, the lead must be swung forward to obtain an up and down cast. Fathoms marked on the lead line are called "marks." The intermediate whole fathoms are called "deeps." In reporting depths it is customary to use these terms as "by the mark

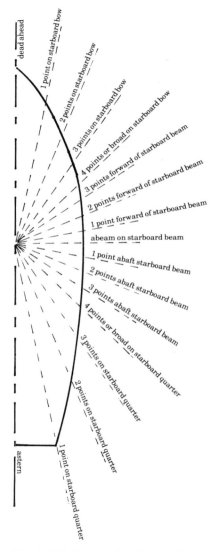

Fig. 41. Relative bearings from a ship.

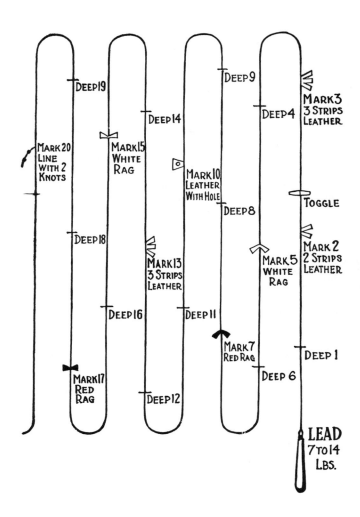

Fig. 42. The markings of a hand-lead line.

five," "deep six," etc. The only fractions of a fathom usually reported are halves and quarters, the customary expression being "and a half, eight," "less a quarter, four," etc.

Blocks and Tackles

Blocks are one of the most important fittings aboard ship. They are either made of wood or metal, and their construction and use should be thoroughly understood. When you are being lowered away in a lifeboat, your life and safety depend upon the blocks in the lifeboat falls. The parts of a wooden block are shown in figure 43. The frame is also known as the shell. The opening between the shell and the top of the sheave is known as the swallow.

Blocks take their name from the number of sheaves; a single block has 1 sheave, a double block has 2, and so on. They are identified by their shape or construction and also by the use or place they occupy aboard ship. The size of the block is governed by the size of the rope to be used with it. The length of a wooden block in inches should be about 3 times the circumference of the fiber rope to be used with it. Blocks for use with wire rope are not so well standardized, but the general Coast Guard rule is that the diameter of the sheave should be 20 times the diameter of the wire.

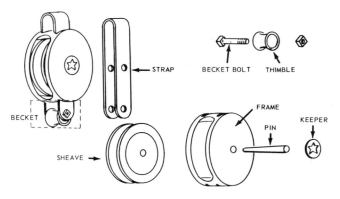

Fig. 43. Parts of a typical wood-framed block.

A tackle or purchase is an assembly of ropes (falls) and blocks used to multiply power or to gain a better lead, as in the use of a single whip, making it easier to handle light loads but gaining no power or mechanical advantage. If the whip is reversed and the block is attached to the weight to be moved, the whip is then called a runner, and the mechanical advantage or power is doubled. An easy way to determine the mechanical advantage is to count the number of parts of line supporting the movable block. A tackle is said to be rigged "to advantage" when hauling on the part of the line that leads through a *movable* block, and " to least advantage" (or "disadvantage") when the hauling end first leads through a *fixed* block. Some of the more common purchases are shown in figure 44.

Strength of Fiber and Wire Rope

Fiber rope. Whenever the question arises as to how strong rope is or what weight it can withstand, the best means of finding out is to go to the manufacturer's specifications. If these specifications cannot be found, the empirical formula given below is useful and is surprisingly accurate. The formula is for Manila rope only, which is the standard. This gives an index for nylon, which is about two and a half times as strong as Manila of the same size. However, it is important to realize that rope which is not new, not stored properly, or is otherwise abused, is less strong than when it left the factory.

The following definitions and abbreviations are used with the formulas:

B = breaking strain (same as tensile strength), in terms of long tons or pounds as specified

C = circumference of rope

SWL or P = safe working load. Safety requires that less stress be placed on the rope or wire than is required to break it, otherwise the gear would frequently be carried away. If the

SWL of Manila is used as 20 percent of B, and B of a 5-inch Manila is 20,250 pounds, then the SWL will be 4,050 pounds.

SF = safety factor—the relationship between B and the SWL. If the SWL of Manila as given in the above example is taken as 20 percent of B, the SF is 5.

Formulas:

$$B = \frac{C^2}{2.5} \qquad \text{or} \qquad B \times 900\, C^2$$

Where B is in long tons (2,240 pounds = 1 long ton) and C is in inches.

Where B is in pounds and C is in inches.

$$SWL = \frac{B}{SF}$$

In this formula, if SWL is in tons, B must be in tons. If SWL is in pounds, B must be in pounds.

Example: What is the breaking strain of 3-inch Manila in tons?

$$B = \frac{C^2}{2.5} = \frac{3^2}{2.5} = \frac{9}{2.5} = 3.6 \text{ long tons}$$

Example: What is the SWL if an SF of 6 is used?

$$SWL = \frac{B}{SF} = \frac{3.6}{6} = .6 \text{ long tons}$$

Formulas for wire rope. The formulas for wire rope are applied in the same manner as for fiber rope. They are:

$$B = 2.5C^2 \text{ or P or } SWL = \frac{C^2}{2.5}$$

Before applying the formulas you must remember:
Wire is measured by the diameter, not by the circumference, as is the case with fiber rope.

The formula assumes a safety factor of 6.25, which is generally used.

The formula holds good only for 6 × 12 plow steel or 6 × 24 cast steel wire. If any other wire is used, the factor of 2.5 will not work. Any seaman knows that the term 6 × 12 means that the wire rope has 6 strands, with 12 wires in each strand.

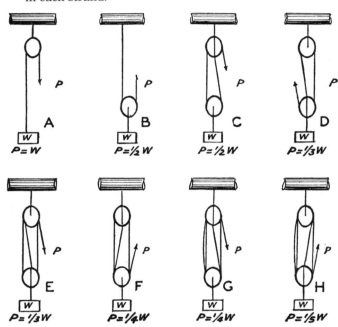

Fig. 44. Common purchases. "P" refers to the force of the pull, and "W" is the weight being lifted. In "A," 1 pound of pull lifts 1 pound of weight. In sketches "B" and "C," 1 pound of pull lifts 2 pounds of weight, and so on. "A" is a single whip and "B" is a single whip inverted or runner. "C" is a gun-tackle purchase rigged to least advantage, and "D" is the same purchase, but rigged to advantage. "E" is a luff tackle rigged to least advantage, and "F" is the same rigged to advantage. (A luff tackle is a combination of one single block and one double block.) "G" is a double or 2-fold purchase rigged to least advantage, and "H" is the same rigged to advantage.

Marlinespike Seamanship

Marlinespike seamanship is a general term that covers all phases of rigging and rope work. It includes the care, handling, knotting, and splicing of both fiber and wire rope of all sizes. A thorough knowledge of rigging and rope work is important to every seaman. The practical part of the able seaman examination may require knowledge about the knots, splices, and canvas work illustrated on the following pages.

Marlinespike seamanship hints. A splice or a knot weakens a line. A spliced line retains 80 to 90% of its strength, but a knot may reduce the strength by 50%.

Extra tucks should be put in splices of nylon or other synthetic ropes. Generally speaking, a splice in Manila, hemp, or sisal should have three full tucks. Nylon or Dacron requires four full tucks and polypropylene should have a minimum of six.

An eye splice in wire rope used for cargo gear should be given three full tucks with whole strands and two tucks with one half the wire from the tucking strand.

Never pull on a kinked wire. You will ruin it. As soon as a kink is noticed, grasp the part of each side of the wire outside the kink and try to enlarge the kink by pushing and working the wire into a loop. Turn the bent portion over, place on a firm object, and push until the kink straightens out as much as possible. Then, the area should be placed on a flat surface and pounded smooth with a wooden mallet.

A shackle is stronger and safer than a hook of the same size. If slings or rope may tend to jump out of the hook, mouse the hook.

When a chain stopper is used to take the weight of a boom, *ease* back the topping lift until the stopper has the weight before throwing off the turns from the warping head. Let the stopper take the weight gradually.

If securing wire rope to cleats or bitts, always use a seizing of marline or other small stuff.

Use blocks large enough for the rope.

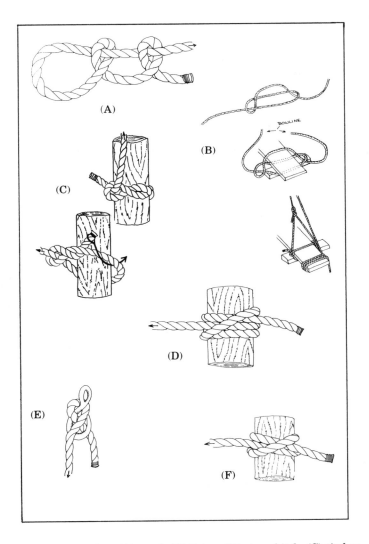

Fig. 45. Hitches: (A) two half hitches, (B) stage hitch, (C) timber hitch, (D) rolling hitch, (E) blackwall hitch, and (F) clove hitch.

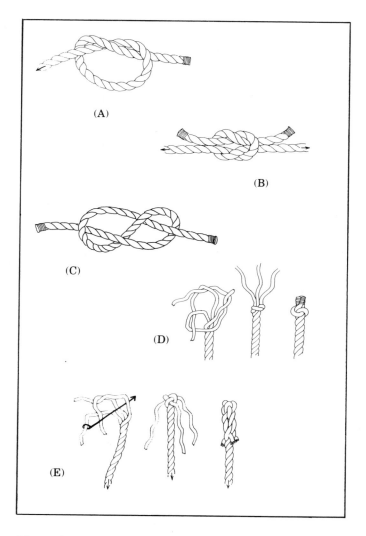

Fig. 46. Knots: (A) overhand knot, (B) square knot, (C) figure eight knot, (D) wall knot, and (E) crown knot.

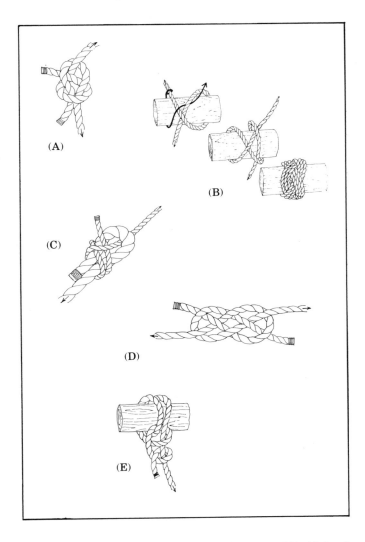

Fig. 47. Bends: (A) single sheet bend, (B) three strand Turk's head, (C) double sheet bend, (D) Carrick bend, and (E) fisherman's bend.

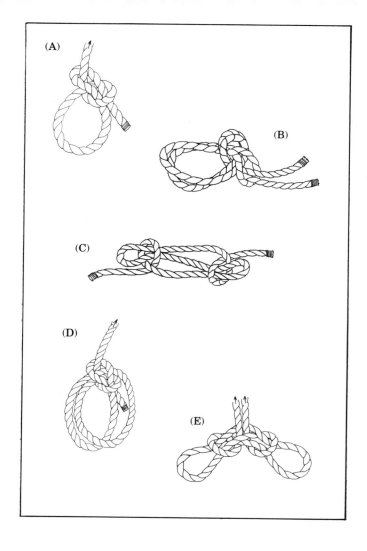

Fig. 48. (A) bowline, (B) bowline on a bight, (C) sheepshank, (D) French bowline, and (E) Spanish bowline.

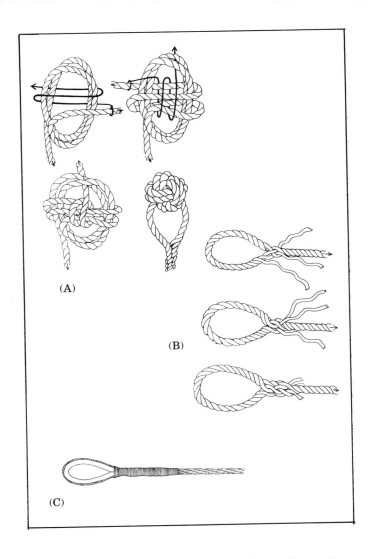

Fig. 49. (A) monkey fist, (B) eye splice, and (C) eye splice in wire.

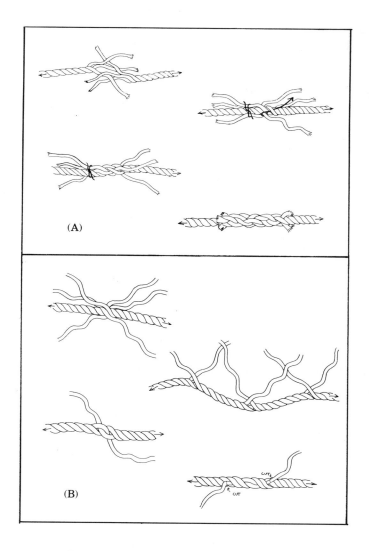

Fig. 50 (A) short splice, and (B) a long splice.

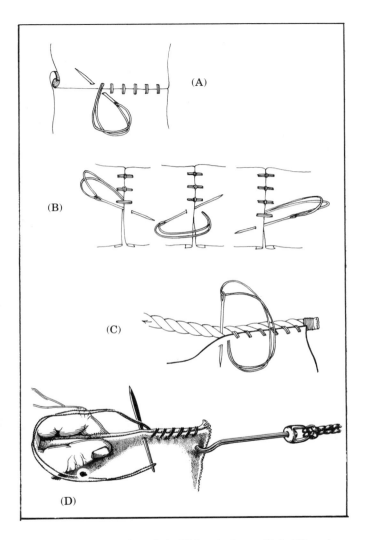

Fig. 51. Stitches: (A) flat stitch, (B) herringbone stitch, (C) sewing a bolt rope to canvas, and (D) round stitching canvas held by a bench hook.

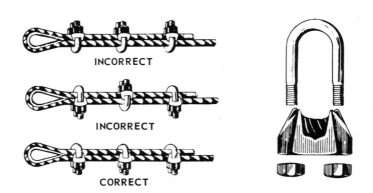

INCORRECT

INCORRECT

CORRECT

Fig. 52. Right and wrong way to use wire clips. Courtesy U.S.

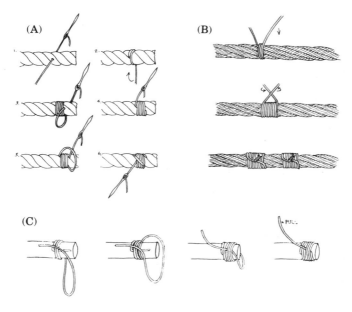

Fig. 53. (A) Palm and needle whipping on a line. (B) Putting temporary seizing on a wire rope. (C) Putting a temporary whipping on a line.

Most rope is right-handed and should be coiled clockwise. Left-handed rope must be coiled counterclockwise or it will kink.

Tarpaulins should be laid with the seams athwartships. The top flap should be aft.

Zinc should be used for a poured basket socket at the end of a wire rope. Babbitt metal or lead is not suitable.

U-bolts used on wire rope clips should fit over the short end of the wire. See figure 52.

Use seizings on the end of wire rope instead of welding. The heat from welding may weaken the wire.

In order to prevent the unlaying of a mooring line, the turns on the windlass should be reversed when unmooring. If, when mooring, the line leads from the chock over the top of the windlass, lead the line under the warping head from the chock. If the line is under tension when unmooring, this will tend to remove the twist.

Pollution

The continuous pollution of our inland and coastal waters has created new and stricter pollution control laws. The mariner must be aware of these laws and must know how to comply with them. He must have the professional skills to carry out his duties without being a hazard to the marine environment. In recent years the pollution laws have become more and more strict. Violations may result in a fine, loss of a license or certificate, or both.

Oil pollution causes serious damage and does it in many ways. It can destroy marine growth, kill birds, ruin beaches, contaminate drinking supplies, and create fire hazards. The hazard of oil pollution is always present in normal operations such as deballasting, bilge cleaning, tank washing, refueling, and transfer operations. While most major spills are caused by large casualties such as collisions or groundings, most minor spills are caused by human error rather than equipment failure.

Pollution is a problem whether heavy or light oil is spilled, even though the slick from light oil tends to vaporize or dissolve. Vapor from light oil is poisonous to sea life even though it cannot be seen.

The law requires that the person in charge of a vessel notify the Coast Guard as soon as he knows of any oil discharge. Failure to do this can lead to a fine of $10,000, a year in jail, or both. Your company can be fined up to $5,000 for a spill, which is still less than the $10,000 charged for not reporting a spill.

The *Code of Federal Regulations* states that only a licensed officer can be "the person in charge" of transfer operations on a tanker. On a tank barge this function may be performed by a certificated tankerman.

Space does not permit an adequate discussion of all regulations concerning pollution, transfer operations, and required procedures, but listing a few will give an idea of their scope:

1. Transfer operations cannot take place unless the vessel's moorings are strong enough to hold in all expected weather conditions and the hoses or arms are long enough to allow the vessel to move at its moorings without strain on the hose or arm.
2. Before a transfer operation, scuppers and drains must be plugged, flange couplings must be properly bolted, and an emergency shutdown system must be available.
3. Before the transfer, a meeting must be held between the person in charge on the vessel and the person in charge at the facility. Both persons in charge must agree to begin the transfer before it may be started.
4. Required lighting must be available for night transfer operations.
5. The Oil Pollution Act of 1990 prohibits the discharge of oil or oily mixtures within the prohibited zone. In general this is 50 miles offshore but may be extended to 100 miles.
6. A tank vessel must have a means of draining or removing discharge oil from each container or enclosed deck area without mixing incompatible products or discharging it into the water.

7. Oil transfer procedures must be printed in a language understood by the crew and permanently posted or available at the fueling or cargo control station.
8. No one may connect, top off, disconnect, or engage in any other critical oil transfer operation unless the person in charge is personally supervising these operations.

Sample Multiple-Choice Questions for the Able Seaman

The able seaman examination given by the Coast Guard consists of a written and a practical test as described in the *Code of Federal Regulations*. The written test is administered in two parts, each consisting of 50 multiple-choice questions in areas which include Rules of the Road, rigging, lifesaving and fire fighting, pollution, and medical care. An overall grade of 70 percent in each part is required in order to pass. If the candidate is deficient in one area (Rules of the Road, for example), and he makes it up in other areas, he is still considered to have passed. He must, however, pass both parts in order to obtain the able seaman endorsement. The international code of signals (H.O. 102) and parts 155, 156, and 157 of Title 33 of the *Code of Federal Regulations* are available in the examining room. Lifeboat and liferaft questions which would duplicate the area covered in the sample questions for lifeboatmen are not included. Answers given are those given in Coast Guard publications. The following questions are taken at random from published banks of Coast Guard Questions. The letter of the correct answer to each question is set in boldface type.

1. An example of a stock anchor is a(n) _____.
   A. articulated anchor
   B. Flipper Delta anchor
   C. hook anchor
   D. Danforth anchor

2. Which part of an anchor actually digs into the bottom?
   A. stock
   B. fluke
   C. shank
   D. crown

3. Buckler plates are _____.
   A. triangular-shaped plates connecting the bull chain
      to the topping lift
   B. metal plates secured over the tops of the hawse pipes
   C. faired shell plates with curvature in two directions
   D. sheets of dunnage used to prevent heavy cargo from
      buckling the deck plates

4. The safety stopper that prevents the anchor cable from
   running free if the cable jumps the wildcat is the
   _____.
   A. riding pawl
   B. devil's claw
   C. buckler plate
   D. spill pipe

5. The recessed areas on a wildcat are called _____.
   A. pawls
   B. sockets
   C. pockets
   D. whelps

6. How is the size of chain determined?
   A. length of link in inches
   B. diameter of metal in link in inches
   C. links per fathom
   D. weight of stud cable in pounds

7. How many turns of wire normally mark either side of
   the shackle 45 fathoms from the anchor?
   A. 1
   B. 2
   C. 3
   D. 4

8. Which of the following is NOT a duty of a lookout?
   A. Refuse to talk to others, except as required by duty.
   B. Remain standing during your watch
   C. Report every sighting
   D. Supervise any deck work going on in the area

9. A lookout should report objects sighted using _____.
   A. true bearings
   B. magnetic bearings
   C. gyro bearings
   D. relative bearings

10. While standing lookout duty at night, a dim light on the horizon will be seen quickest by looking: _____.
    A. at an area just a little below the horizon
    B. at the horizon, where the sky and the water appears to meet
    C. a little above the horizon
    D. well below the horizon line

11. You are standing wheelwatch on entering port, and the Master gives you a rudder command that conflicts with a rudder command from the Pilot. What should you do?
    A. Obey the Pilot.
    B. Obey the Master.
    C. Ask the Pilot for guidance.
    D. Bring the rudder to midships

12. When relieving the helm, the new helmsman should know the _____.
    A. gyro error
    B. course per magnetic steering compass
    C. variation
    D. maximum rudder angle previously used

13. You are standing the wheelwatch when you hear the cry, "Man overboard starboard side." You should be ready to:
    A. give full right rudder
    B. give full left rudder
    C. put the rudder amidships
    D. throw a lifering to mark the spot

14. The helm command, "meet her" means _____.
    A. steer more carefully
    B. use the rudder to check the swing
    C. decrease the existing rudder angle
    D. note the course and steady on that bearing

15. The "Iron Mike" is a(n) _____.
    A. pilot
    B. speaker
    C. standby wheel
    D. automatic pilot

16. Your ship is steaming at night with the gyropilot engaged when you notice that the vessel's course is slowly changing to the right. Which of the following actions should you take FIRST?
    A. Notify the engine room of the steering malfunction.
    B. Change to telemotor (or other alternate steering system)
    C. Call the Master
    D. Send the quartermaster to the emergency steering station

17. You are on watch aboard a vessel heading NW with the wind from dead ahead, in heavy seas. You notice a man fall overboard from the starboard bow. Which of the following actions would NOT be appropriate?
    A. Hard right rudder
    B. Throw a life buoy to the man, if possible
    C. Send a man aloft
    D. Get the port boat ready

18. Which of the following is NOT an advantage of the Williamson turn?
    A. In a large vessel (VLCC) much of the headway will be lost thereby requiring little astern maneuvering.
    B. When the turn is completed, the vessel will be on the original track line.

C. The initial actions are taken at well defined points and reduce the need for individual judgement.

D. The turn will return the vessel to the man's location in the shortest possible time.

19. A rescue helicopter hoist area would preferably have a minimum radius of at least _____.
    A. 6 feet of clear deck
    B. 10 feet of clear deck
    C. 25 feet of clear deck
    D. 50 feet of clear deck

20. When anchoring a vessel under normal conditions, what scope of chain is recommended?
    A. four times the depth of water
    B. two and one-half times the depth of water
    C. five to seven times the depth of water
    D. fifteen times the depth of water.

21. The strongest of the natural fibers is _____.
    A. cotton
    B. hemp
    C. Manila
    D. sisal

22. Line is called "small stuff" if its circumference is less than _____.
    A. ½ "
    B. ¾ "
    C. 1"
    D. 1¾ "

23. As you hold a piece of manila line vertically in front of you, the strands run from the lower left to the upper right. What type of line is this?
    A. right-hand laid
    B. cable-laid
    C. sennet-laid
    D. water-laid

24. In order to clean a mooring line that is full of mud and sand, the line should be _____.
    A. hosed down with fresh water
    B. hosed down with salt water
    C. scrubbed with detergent and water
    D. steam cleaned with high pressure steam

25. Which of the following types of line would BEST be able to withstand sudden shock loads?
    A. polypropylene
    B. nylon
    C. dacron
    D. Manila

26. The critical point in nylon line elongation is considered to be:
    A. 20%
    B. 30%
    C. 40%
    D. 50%

27. A mooring line is described as being 6 × 24, 1¾ inch wire rope. What do the above numbers refer to?
    A. strands, yarns, circumference
    B. strands, wires, diameter
    C. wires, yarns, diameter
    D. strands, circumference, wires

28. A rope made of a combination of wire and fiber is known as _____.
    A. independent
    B. lang lay
    C. preformed
    D. spring lay

29. Galvanizing would NOT be suitable for protecting a wire rope which is used for _____.
    A. cargo runners
    B. mooring wires

C. shrouds

D. stays

30. The ultimate or maximum strength of a wire rope is referred to as the _____.
    A. operating strength
    B. working load
    C. breaking strength
    D. lifting load

31. If kinking results while wire rope is being coiled clockwise, you should _____.
    A. coil it counter clockwise
    B. not coil it
    C. take a turn under
    D. twist out the kinks under a strain

32. Mousing a cargo hook with marline or small line _____.
    A. increases the lifting capacity of the hook
    B. protects the hook from the sling ring
    C. prevents the sling ring from coming out of the hook
    D. all of the above

33. When rigging a bosun's chair on a stay with a shackle, _____.
    A. mouse the shackle to the chair
    B. never allow the shackle pin to ride on the stay
    C. secure it with small stuff
    D. seize the end of the shackle

34. A mooring line that checks forward motion of a vessel at a pier is a _____.
    A. bow line
    B. forward bow line
    C. stern line
    D. stern breast line

35. Which mooring line is likely to undergo the most strain when docking a ship under normal conditions?
    A. bow line
    B. breast line
    C. spring line
    D. stern line

36. To "belay" a line means _____.
    A. coil it down
    B. heave it taut
    C. stow it below
    D. secure it to a cleat

37. You are handling a mooring line and you are instructed to "Check the line." What should be done?
    A. You should ensure the bight is not fouled between the ship and dock by taking up the slack.
    B. The line is paid out smartly and kept free for running.
    C. The line should be secured by adding more turns and then the area should be cleared.
    D. The line is surged so that it maintains a strain without parting.

38. When a line is laid down in loose, looping figure eights, it is said to be _____.
    A. faked
    B. flemished
    C. coiled
    D. chined

39. A "figure-eight" knot is used to _____.
    A. be a stopper
    B. shorten a line
    C. join lines of equal size
    D. keep a line from passing through a sheave

40. What knot or bend is used to tie a small line to a larger one?
    A. becket bend

B. bowline
C. clove hitch
D. lark's head

41. The knot used to join two lines or two large hawsers for towing is called a _____.
    A. square knot
    B. carrick bend
    C. sheet bend
    D. bowline

42. You need to make a fixed loop at the end of a line in order to use the line as a mooring line. You have no time to make a splice. Which knot should you use?
    A. bowline
    B. figure-eight
    C. overhand
    D. round-turn and two half hitches

43. A "whipping" is _____.
    A. a messenger
    B. a stopper for nylon line
    C. a U-bolt for securing a cargo whip to the winch drum
    D. twine tied around a rope end

44. A splice that can be used in running rigging, where the line will pass through blocks, is a _____.
    A. short splice
    B. long splice
    C. back splice
    D. spindle splice

45. The correct way to make an eye in a wire rope with clips is to place the clips with the _____.
    A. first and third U-bolts on the bitter end and the second U-bolt on the standing part
    B. first and third U-bolts on the standing part and the second U-bolt on the bitter end
    C. U-bolts of all clips on the bitter end
    D. U-bolts of all clips on the standing part

46. What is the name of this tackle?
    A. whip
    B. one fold purchase
    C. gun tackle
    D. runner

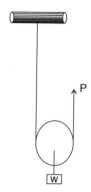

47. A snatch block would most likely be used as a _____.
    A. boat fall
    B. fairlead
    C. riding pawl
    D. topping lift

48. What size block shell should be used with a 4-inch Manila line?
    A. 8"
    B. 12"
    C. 16"
    D. 24"

49. Unless extremely flexible wire rope is used, the sheave diameter should always be as large as possible, but should NEVER be less than _____.
    A. 20 times the rope diameter
    B. 10 times the rope diameter
    C. 2 times the rope diameter
    D. the rope diameter

50. When a block and tackle is "rove to advantage," this means that the _____.
    A. blocks have been overhauled
    B. hauling parts of two tackles are attached
    C. hauling part leads through the movable block
    D. hauling part leads through the standing block

51. Most minor spills of oil products are caused by _____.
    A. equipment failure
    B. human error
    C. major casualties
    D. unforeseeable circumstances

52. Heavy fuel oils when spilled are _____.
    A. more harmful to sea life than lighter oils
    B. easier to clean up than lighter refined oils
    C. less harmful to sea life than lighter oils
    D. not a real threat to marine life

53. Which statement is TRUE of a gasoline spill?
    A. It is visible for a shorter time than a fuel oil spill.
    B. It is not covered by pollution laws.
    C. It does little harm to marine life.
    D. It will sink more rapidly than crude oil.

54. In reference to accidental oil pollution, the most critical time during bunkering is when _____.
    A. you first start to receive fuel
    B. hoses are being blown down
    C. final topping off is occurring
    D. hoses are being disconnected

55. Except in rare cases, it is impossible to extinguish a shipboard fire by _____.
    A. removing the heat
    B. removing the oxygen
    C. removing the fuel
    D. interrupting the chain reaction

56. What is required in addition to the heat, fuel, and oxygen of the fire triangle to have a fire?
   A. smoke
   B. electricity
   C. pressure
   D. chain reaction

57. The spread of fire is prevented by _____.
   A. cooling surfaces adjacent to the fire
   B. removing combustibles from the endangered area
   C. shutting off the oxygen supply
   D. all of the above

58. What, when removed, will result in the extinguishment of a fire?
   A. nitrogen
   B. sodium
   C. oxygen
   D. carbon dioxide

59. All of the following are part of the fire triangle except _____.
   A. heat
   B. oxygen
   C. electricity
   D. fuel

60. If ignited, which material would be a class B fire?
   A. magnesium
   B. paper
   C. wood
   D. diesel oil

61. A triangular daymark would be colored _____.
   A. red
   B. red and white
   C. green
   D. green and white

62. Deviation is caused by _____.
    A. changes in the earth's magnetic field
    B. nearby magnetic land masses or mineral deposits
    C. magnetic influence inherent to that particular vessel
    D. all of the above

63. What is the mark on a lead line indicating 10 fathoms?
    A. one knot
    B. one strip of leather
    C. leather with a hole
    D. no marking

64. The four standard light colors used for lighted aids to navigation are red, green, white and _____.
    A. purple
    B. orange
    C. blue
    D. yellow

65. The magnetic compass error which changes with the geographical location of your vessel is called _____.
    A. deviation
    B. variation
    C. compensation
    D. differentiation

66. First aid means _____.
    A. medical treatment of accident
    B. setting of broken bones
    C. emergency treatment at the scene of the injury
    D. dosage of medications

67. When giving first aid, you should understand how to conduct primary and secondary surveys and know _____.
    A. which medications to prescribe
    B. how to diagnose an illness from symptoms
    C. the limits of your capabilities
    D. how to set broken bones

68. In managing a situation involving multiple injuries, the
    rescuer must be able to _____.
    A. provide the necessary medication
    B. rapidly evaluate the seriousness of obvious injuries
    C. accurately diagnose the ailment or injury
    D. prescribe treatment for the victim

69. A compound fracture is a fracture _____.
    A. in which more than one bone is broken
    B. in which the same bone is broken in more than one
       place
    C. which is never accompanied by internal bleeding
    D. in which the bone may be visible

70. BOTH INTERNATIONAL & INLAND. If you saw
    flames aboard a vessel but could see the vessel was not
    on fire, you would know that _____.
    A. the crew was trying to get warm
    B. the vessel required immediate assistance
    C. the vessel was attempting to attract the attention of
       a pilot boat
    D. the vessel was being illuminated for identification
       by aircraft

71. BOTH INTERNATIONAL & INLAND. Five or more
    short blasts on a vessel's whistle indicates that she is

    _____.
    A. in doubt that another vessel is taking sufficient
       action to avoid collision
    B. altering course to starboard
    C. altering course to port
    D. the stand-on vessel and will maintain course and
       speed

72. BOTH INTERNATIONAL & INLAND. You are watch-
    ing another vessel and its compass bearing does not
    change. This would indicate that _____.
    A. you are the stand-on vessel
    B. a risk of collision exists

C. a special circumstances situation exists

D. the other vessel is dead in the water

73. BOTH INTERNATIONAL & INLAND. While underway and making way your vessel enters fog. What fog signal should you sound every two minutes?

A. one prolonged blast

B. two prolonged blasts

C. three short blasts

D. a prolonged blast and two short blasts

74. BOTH INTERNATIONAL & INLAND. When two power-driven vessels are meeting head-on and there is a risk of collision, each shall _____.

A. stop her engines

B. alter course to starboard

C. sound the danger signal

D. back down

75. A true bearing of a charted object, when plotted on a chart, will establish a _____.

A. fix

B. line of position

C. relative bearing

D. range

5. The Qualified Member of the Engine Department

The following information concerning requirements and certification as a qualified member of the engine department is reproduced from the *Code of Federal Regulations: Title 46—Shipping,* Subparts 12.15 to 12.17 (Washington, D.C.: U.S. Government Printing Office, 1999).

Subpart 12.15—Qualified Member of the Engine Department

§ 12.15-1 Certification required.

(a) Every person employed in a rating as qualified member of the engine department on any United States vessel requiring certificated qualified members of the engine department shall produce a certificate as qualified member of the engine department to the shipping commissioner, United States Collector or Deputy Collector of Customs, or master before signing articles of agreement.

(b) No certificate as qualified member of the engine department is required of any person employed on any unrigged vessel, except seagoing barges.

§ 12.15-3 General requirements.

(a) A qualified member of the engine department is any person below the rating of licensed officer and above the rating of coal passer or wiper, who holds a certificate of service as such qualified member of the engine department issued by the Coast Guard or predecessor authority.

(b) For purposes of administering this part the rating of "assistant electrician" is considered a rating not above that of coal passer or wiper, but equal thereto.

(c) An applicant, to be eligible for certification as qualified member of the engine department, shall be able to speak and understand the English language as would be required in the rating of qualified member of the engine department and in an emergency aboard ship.

(d) After July 31, 1998, an STCW endorsement valid for any period on or after February 1, 2002, will be issued or renewed only when the candidate for certification as a qualified member of the engine department also produces satisfactory evidence, on the basis of assessment of a practical demonstration of skills and abilities, of having achieved or maintained within the previous 5 years the minimum standards of competence for the following 4 area of basis safety:

(1) Personal survival techniques as set out in table A-VI/1-1 of the STCW Code.

(2) Fire prevention and fire-fighting as set out in table A-VI/1-2 of the STCW Code.

(3) Elementary first aid as set out in table A-VI/1-3 of the STCW Code.

(4) Personal safety and social responsibilities as set out in table A-VI/1-4 of the STCW Code.

(e) After July 31, 1998 an STCW endorsement that is valid for any period on or after February 1, 2002, will be issued or renewed only when the candidate for certification as a qualified member of the engine department meets the standards of competence set out in STCW Regulation III/4 and Section A-III/4 of the STCW Code, if the candidate will be serving as a rating forming part of a watch in a manned engine-room, or designated to perform duties in a periodically unmanned engine-room, on a seagoing ship driven by main propulsion machinery of 750 kW [1,000 hp] propulsion power or more.

[CGFR 65-50, 30 FR 16640, Dec. 30, 1965, as amended by CGD 95-062, 62 FR 34538, June 26, 1997]

§ 12.15-5 Physical requirements.

(a) An applicant for a certificate of service as a qualified member of the engine department shall present a certificate of a medical officer of the United States Public Health Service, or other reputable physician attesting that his eyesight, hearing, and physical condition are such that he can perform the duties required of a qualified member of the engine department.

(b) The medical examination for qualified member of the engine department is the same as for an original license as engineer, as set forth in § 10.02-5 of this subchapter. If the applicant is in possession of an unexpired license, the Officer in Charge, Marine Inspection, may waive the requirement for a physical examination.

(c) An applicant holding a certificate of service for a particular rating as qualified member of the engine department and desiring certification for another rating covered by this same form of certificate may qualify therefor without a physical examination unless the Officer in Charge, Marine Inspection, finds that the applicant obviously suffers from some physical or mental infirmity to a degree that would render him incompetent to perform the ordinary duties of a qualified member of the engine department. In this event the applicant shall be required to undergo an examination to determine his competency.

[CGFR 65-50, 30 FR 16640, Dec. 30, 1965, as amended by USCG-1998-4442, 63 FR 52189, Sept. 30, 1998]

§ 12.15-7 Service or training requirements.

(a) An applicant for a certificate of service as qualified member of the engine department shall furnish the Coast Guard proof of qualification based on six months' service in a rating at least equal to that of wiper or coal passer.

(b) Training programs approved by the Commandant may be substituted for the required service at sea in accordance with the following:

(1) A graduate of a school ship may be rated as qualified member of the engine department upon satisfactory completion of the course of instruction. For this purpose, "school ship" is interpreted to mean an institution which offers a complete course of instruction, including a period of sea training, in the skills appropriate to the rating of qualified member of the engine department.

(2) Training programs other than those classified as a school ship may be substituted for up to one-half of the required service at sea.

(c) To qualify to receive an STCW endorsement for service as a "rating forming part of a watch in a manned engine-room or designated to perform duties in a periodically unmanned engine-room" on a seagoing vessel driven by main propulsion machinery 750 kW [1,000 hp] propulsion power or more, an applicant shall prove seagoing service that includes training and experience associated with engine-room watchkeeping and involves the performance of duties carried out under the direct supervision of a qualified engineer officer or a member of a qualified rating. The training must establish that the applicant has achieved the standard of competence prescribed in table A-III/4 of the STCW Code, in accordance with the methods of demonstrating competence and the criteria for evaluating competence specified in that table.

[CGD 80-131, 45 FR 69241, Oct. 20, 1980, as amended by CGD 95-072, 60 FR 50460, Sept. 29, 1995; CGD 95-062, 62 FR 34538, June 26, 1997; CGD 95-062, 62 FR 40140, July 25, 1997; USCG-1998-4442, 63 FR 52189, Sept. 30, 1998]

§ 12.15-9 Examination requirements. (10-1-99 Edition)

(a) Applicants for certification as qualified members of the engine department in the ratings of oiler, watertender, fireman, deck engineer, refrigerator engineer, junior engineer, electrician, and machinist shall be examined orally or in writing and only in the English language on the subjects listed in paragraph (b) of this section. The applicant's general knowledge of the subjects must be sufficient to satisfy the examiner that he is qualified to perform the duties of the rating for which he makes application.

(b) List of subjects required:

Subjects	Machinist	Refrigerating engineer	Fireman/Watertender	Oiler	Electrician	Junior engineer	Deck engineer
1. Application, maintenance, and use of hand tools and measuring instruments	x	x	x	x	x	x	x

Subjects	Machinist	Refrigerating engineer	Fireman/Watertender	Oiler	Electrician	Junior engineer	Deck engineer
2. Uses of babbitt, copper, brass, steel, and other metals	x	x	x	x	x	x	x
3. Methods of measuring pipe, pipe fittings, sheet metal, machine bolts and nuts, packing, etc.	x	x	x	x	x	x	x
4. Operation and maintenance of mechanical remote control equipment	x		x	x	x	x	x
5. Precautions to be taken for the prevention of fire and the proper use of firefighting equipment	x	x	x	x	x	x	x
6. Principles of mechanical refrigeration; and functions, operation, and maintenance of various machines and parts of the systems		x		x		x	
7. Knowledge of piping systems as used in ammonia, freon, and CO_2, including testing for leaks, operation of bypasses, and making up of joints		x				x	
8. Safety precautions to be observed in the operation of various refrigerating systems, including storage of refrigerants, and the use of gas masks and firefighting equipment	x	x	x	x	x	x	x
9. Combustion of fuels, proper temperature, pressures, and atomization			x	x		x	
10. Operation of the fuel oil system on oil burning boilers, including the transfer and storage of fuel oil			x	x		x	x
11. Hazards involved and the precautions taken against accumulation of oil in furnaces, bilges, floorplates, and tank tops; flarebacks, leaks in fuel oil heaters, clogged strainers and burner tips	x	x	x	x	x	x	x
12. Precautions necessary when filling empty boilers, starting up the fuel oil burning system, and raising steam from a cold boiler			x	x		x	

Subject	Machinist	Refrigerating engineer	Fireman/Watertender	Oiler	Electrician	Junior engineer	Deck engineer
13. The function, operation, and maintenance of the various engineroom auxiliaries	x	x	x	x	x	x	
14. Proper operation of the various types of lubricating systems	x	x	x	x	x	x	x
15. Safety precautions to be observed in connection with the operation of engineroom auxiliaries, electrical machinery, and switchboard equipment	x	x	x	x	x	x	x
16. The function, operation, and maintenance of the bilge, ballast, fire, freshwater, sanitary, and lubricating systems	x	x	x	x		x	x
17. Proper care of spare machine parts and idle equipment	x	x	x	x	x	x	x
18. The procedure in preparing a turbine, reciprocating, or Diesel engine for standby; also the procedure in securing			x	x		x	
19. Operation and maintenance of the equipment necessary for the supply of water to boilers, the dangers of high and low water and remedial action			x	x		x	
20. Operation, location, and maintenance of the various boiler fittings and accessories	x		x	x		x	
21. The practical application and solution of basic electrical calculations (Ohm's law, power formula, etc.					x	x	x
22. Electrical wiring circuits of the various two-wire and three-wire D.C. systems and the various single-phase and polyphase A.C. systems					x	x	x
23. Application and characteristics of parallel and series circuits					x	x	x
24. Application and maintenance of electrical meters and instruments					x	x	x

Subject	Machinist	Refrigerating engineer	Fireman/Watertender	Oiler	Electrician	Junior engineer	Deck engineer
25. The maintenance and installation of lighting and power wiring involving testing for, locating, and correcting grounds, short circuits and open circuits, and making splices					x	x	x
26. The operation and maintenance of the various types of generators and motors, both A.C. and D.C.					x	x	x
27. Operation, installation, and maintenance of the various types of electrical controls and safety devices					x	x	x
28. Testing and maintenance of special electrical equipment, such as telegraphs, telephones, alarm systems, fire-detecting systems, and rudder angle indicators					x	x	
29. Rules and Regulations and requirements for installation, repair, and maintenance of electrical wiring and equipment installed aboard ships.					x	x	x
29a. Pollution laws and regulations, procedures for discharge containment and cleanup, and methods for disposal of sludge and waste from cargo and fueling operations	x	x	x	x	x	x	
30. Such further examination of a nonmathematical character as the Officer in Charge, Marine Inspection, may consider necessary to establish the applicant's proficiency	x	x	x	x	x	x	x

(c) Each applicant for certification as qualified member of the engine department in the rating of pumpman shall, by oral or other examination, demonstrate sufficient knowledge of the subjects peculiar to that rating to satisfy the Officer in Charge, Marine Inspection, that he or she is qualified to perform the duties of that rating.

(d) Applicants for certification as qualified members of the engine department in the rating of deck engine mechanic or engineman, who have proved eligibility for such endorsement under either § 12.15-13 or § 12.15-15, will not be required to take a written or oral examination for such ratings.

[CGFR 65-50, 30 FR 16640, Dec. 30, 1965, as amended by CGFR 66-46, 31 FR 13649, Oct. 22, 1966; CGD 71-161R, 37 FR 28263, Dec. 21, 1972; CGD 74-75, 42 FR 24741, May 16, 1977; CGD 94-029, 61 FR 47064, Sept. 6, 1996]

§ 12.15-11 General provisions respecting merchant mariner's documents endorsed as qualified member of the engine department.

The holder of a merchant mariner's document endorsed with one or more qualified member of the engine department ratings may serve in any unqualified rating in the engine department without obtaining an additional endorsement. This does not mean that an endorsement of one qualified member of the engine department rating authorizes the holder to serve in all qualified member of the engine department ratings. Each qualified member of the engine department rating for which a holder of a merchant mariner's document is qualified must be endorsed separately. When, however, the applicant qualifies for all ratings covered by a certificate as a qualified member of the engine department, the certification may read "QMED—any rating." The ratings are as follows:

(a) Refrigerating engineer

(b) Oiler

(c) Deck engineer

(d) Fireman/ Watertender

(e) Junior engineer

(f) Electrician

(g) Machinist

(h) Pumpman

(i) Deck engine mechanic

(j) Engineman

(80 Stat. 973; 46 U.S.C 133)

[CGFR 65-50, 30 FR 16640, Dec. 30, 1965, as amended by CGFR 66-46, 31 FR 13649, Oct. 22, 1966; CGD 74-45, 42 FR 24741, May 16, 1977]

§ 12.15-13 Deck engine mechanic.

(a) An applicant for a certificate as "deck engine mechanic" shall be a person holding a merchant mariner's document endorsed as "junior engineer." The applicant shall be eligible for such certification upon furnishing one of the following:

(1) Satisfactory documentary evidence of sea service of 6 months in the rating of "junior engineer" on steam vessels of 4,000 horsepower or over; or,

(2) Documentary evidence from an operator of an automated vessel that he has completed satisfactorily at least 4 weeks indoctrination and training in the engine department of an automated steam vessel of 4,000 horsepower or over; or,

(3) Satisfactory completion of a course of training for "deck engine mechanic" acceptable to the Commanding Officer, National Maritime Center.

(b) The Officer in Charge, Marine Inspection, who is satisfied that an applicant for the rating of "deck engine mechanic" meets the requirements specified in this section, will endorse this rating on the current merchant mariner's document held by the applicant.

(c) Any holder of a merchant mariner's document endorsed for "any unlicensed rating in the engine department" or "QMED—any rating" is qualified as a "deck engine mechanic" and that endorsement will not be entered on his document.

[CGFR 66-46, 31 FR 13649, Oct. 22, 1966, as amended by CGD 95-072, 60 FR 50460, Sept. 29, 1995; CGD 95-028, 62 FR 51196, Sept. 30, 1997; USCG-1998-4442, 63 FR 52189, Sept. 30, 1998]

§ 12.15-15 Engineman.

(a) An applicant for a certificate as "engineman" shall be a person holding a merchant mariner's document endorsed as "fireman/watertender" and "oiler," or "junior engineer." The applicant shall be eligible for such certification upon furnishing one of the following:

(1) Satisfactory documentary evidence of sea service of 6 months in any one or combination of "junior engineer," "fireman/watertender" or "oiler" on steam vessels of 4,000 horsepower or over; or,

(2) Documentary evidence from an operator of a "partially automated" steam vessel that he has completed satisfactorily at least 2 weeks indoctrination and training in the engine department of a "partially automated" steam vessel of 4,000 horsepower or over; or

(3) Satisfactory completion of a course of training for "engineman" acceptable to the Commanding Officer, National Maritime Center.

(b) The Officer in Charge, Marine Inspection, who is satisfied that an applicant for the rating of "engineman" meets the requirements specified in this section, will endorse this rating on the current merchant mariner's document held by the applicant.

(c) Any holder of a merchant mariner's document endorsed for "any unlicensed rating in the engine department," "QMED—any rating" or "deck engine mechanic" is qualified as an "engineman" and that endorsement will not be entered on his document.

[CGFR 66-46, 31 FR 13650, Oct. 22, 1966, as amended by CGD 95-072, 60 FR 50460, Sept. 29, 1995; CGD 95-028, 62 FR 51196, Sept. 30, 1997; USCG–1998–4442, 63 FR 52189, Sept. 30, 1998]

Subpart 12.17—General Requirements for Issuance of Temporary Certificates of Service for Qualified Member of the Engine Department on Offshore Supply Vessels

SOURCE: CGD 80-131, 45 FR 69241, Oct. 20, 1980, unless otherwise noted.

EFFECTIVE DATE NOTE: At 62 FR 51196, Sept. 30, 1997, subpart 12.17, consisting of §§ 12.17–1 through 12.17–20 was removed, effective Oct. 30, 1997.

§ 12.17-1 Eligibility.

A person is eligible for a temporary certificate of service as Qualified Member of the Engine Department for offshore supply vessels if:

(a) Application is made on or before January 6,1981; and,

(b) The applicant was serving in an equivalent capacity on board an offshore supply vessel as defined by 46 U.S.C. 404-1, on or before January 1, 1979.

§ 12.17-5 Application procedure.

(a) A person may apply for a temporary certificate of service as Qualified Member of the Engine Department at any Coast Guard Marine Inspection or Marine Safety Office.

(b) Application shall be made upon Coast Guard Form "Application for Temporary License or Certificate of Service for Crews of Offshore Supply Vessels."

§ 12.17-7 Service under an acknowledgment of application.

(a) Upon receipt of the completed application, the Officer in Charge, Marine Inspection, issues an "acknowledgment of application" to the applicant. Upon receipt of this acknowledgment, the applicant is deemed to be in compliance with the statutes dealing with certification of merchant marine personnel pending issuance of a temporary certificate or expiration of the acknowledgment of application.

(b) An acknowledgment of application is subject to suspension and revocation on the same grounds and procedures as provided by 46 U.S.C. 239.

(c) An acknowledgment of application shall remain valid until October 7, 1982.

§ 12.17-10 Issuance of temporary certificates of service.

(a) An Officer in Charge, Marine Inspection, may issue temporary certificates of service on or before October 6, 1982, to persons who have applied under § 12.17-5 and meet the requirements of § 12.17-15.

(b) Temporary certificates of service issued under the provisions of this part:

(1) Authorize service only upon offshore supply vessels;

(2) Remain valid for a period of three years from the date of issuance;

(3) May not be raised in grade;

(4) Are not renewable except for replacement occasioned by loss; and,

(5) Are subject to suspension and revocation on the same grounds and procedures as provided by 46 U.S.C. 239.

(c) Authority to issue temporary certificates of service of Qualified Member of the Engine Department expires on October 7, 1982.

§ 12.17-15 Requirements for temporary certificates of service.

(a) An applicant for a temporary certificate of service as Qualified Member of the Engine Department must meet the:

(1) Physical requirements of § 12.15-5; and

(2) The citizenship requirements of § 12.02-13 and § 12.02-14 before such certificate of service shall be issued.

(b) An applicant for a temporary certificate of service shall present to the Officer in Charge, Marine Inspection, letters, discharges, or other official documents certifying the amount and character of sea service, and the names of the vessels on which acquired. The Officer in Charge, Marine Inspection, must be satisfied as to the bona fides of all evidence of sea service or training presented and may reject any evidence not considered to be authentic or which does not sufficiently outline the amount, type and character of service.

(c) The minimum service required to obtain a temporary certificate of service as Qualified Member of the Engine Department is 95 days of service as chief engineer, assistant engineer or qualified member of the engine department on board offshore supply vessels.

NOTE: A twelve hour work day is equivalent to one day of the above service requirements. An eight hour work day is equivalent to two thirds of a service day.

(d) Service as chief engineer, assistant engineer or qualified member of the engine department on board offshore supply vessels while holding the acknowledgment of application issued in accordance with § 12.17-7 may be utilized to meet the sea service requirements of paragraph (c) of this section.

§ 12.17-20 Possession of temporary certificate of service or acknowledgment of application.

An individual employed in a certificated capacity upon an offshore supply vessel under a valid temporary certificate or acknowledgment of application must have the document in his or her possession and available for examination at all times.

References

The following publications are suggested for further study.

Bowditch, Nathaniel (original author). *American Practical Navigator* (Pub. No. 9). Washington, D.C.: United States Government Printing Office, 1989.

Hayler, William B., John M. Keever, and Paul M. Seiler, eds. *American Merchant Seaman's Manual.* 6th ed. Centreville, Md.: Cornell Maritime Press, 1981.

International Code of Signals. Suitland, Md.: Defense Mapping Agency, 1990.

Krabenschmidt, Dale. *Marine Firefighting Training Manual.* Oakland, Calif.: Military Sealift Command, Pacific, 1980.

Maloney, Elbert S., ed. *Dutton's Navigation and Piloting.* 14th ed. Annapolis, Md.: Naval Institute Press, 1985.

Manual for the Safe Handling of Flammable and Combustible Liquids and Other Hazardous Products (CG-174), Department of Transportation, U.S. Coast Guard, 1976.

Marine Fire Prevention, Firefighting, and Fire Safety. Washington, D.C.: Department of Commerce, Maritime Administration, 1988.

Marton, G.S. *Tanker Operations: A Handbook for the Ship's Officer.* 3d ed. Centreville, Md.: Cornell Maritime Press, 1992.

Navigation Rules, International-Inland. Washington, D.C.: Department of Transportation, United States Coast Guard, 1999.

Sauerbier, Charles L., and Robert J. Meurn. *Marine Cargo Operations.* 2d ed. New York: John Wiley & Sons, 1985.

Shipboard Guide for Pollution-Free Operations. Washington, D.C.: Department of Commerce, 1976.

Ship's Medicine Chest and Medical Aid at Sea. Washington, D.C.: United States Department of Health, Education and Welfare, 1987.

Appendix:
United States Coast Guard
Regional Examination Centers
(RECs)

Examinations for the ratings for which this book has been prepared are given at each of the twenty-one Coast Guard Regional Examination Centers (RECs) listed below. RECs are prepared not only to administer examinations, but also to provide information about procedures and about Coast Guard services available at other facilities.

It is suggested that candidates write or phone their nearest REC for specific information.

Alaska

U.S. Coast Guard, Marine Safety Office (REC)
510 L. Street, Suite 100
Anchorage, AK 99501-1946
(907) 271-6736

U.S. Coast Guard, Marine Safety Office (REC)
2760 Sherwood Lane, Suite 2A
Juneau, AK 99801-8545
(907) 463-2458

U.S. Coast Guard, Marine Safety Office (REC)
2030 Sealevel Dr., Suite 203
Ketchikan, AK 99901
(907) 225-4496

California

U.S. Coast Guard, Marine Safety Office (REC)
Building 14, Room 109, Coast Guard Island
San Francisco Bay, CA 94501-5100
(510) 437-3095

U.S. Coast Guard, Marine Safety Office (REC)
165 N. Pico Avenue
Long Beach, CA 90802-1096
(562) 980-4485

Florida

U.S. Coast Guard, Marine Safety Office (REC)
Claude Pepper Federal Bldg., 6th Floor
51 S.W. First Avenue
Miami, FL 33130-1609
(305) 536-6548

Hawaii

U.S. Coast Guard, Marine Safety Office (REC)
433 Ala Moana Boulevard, Rm. 1
Honolulu, HI 96813-4909
(808) 522-8264

Louisiana

U.S. Coast Guard, Marine Safety Office (REC)
9820 Lake Forest Blvd., Suite P
New Orleans, LA 70127-3077
(504) 589-6183

Maryland

U.S. Coast Guard, Marine Safety Office (REC)
U.S. Custom House
40 S. Gay Street
Baltimore, MD 21202-4022
(410) 962-5132

Massachusetts

U.S. Coast Guard, Marine Safety Office (REC)
455 Commercial Street
Boston, MA 02109-1045
(617) 223-3040

Missouri

U.S. Coast Guard, Marine Safety Office (REC)
1222 Spruce Street, Suite 8.104E
St. Louis, MO 63103-2835
(314) 539-3091

New York

U.S. Coast Guard, Marine Inspection Office (REC)
Battery Park Bldg.
New York, NY 10004-8545
(212) 668-7492

Ohio

U.S. Coast Guard, Marine Safety Office (REC)
Federal Bldg., Rm. 501
234 Summit Street
Toledo, OH 43604-1590
(419) 259-6395

Oregon

U.S. Coast Guard, Marine Safety Office (REC)
6767 N. Basin Avenue
Portland, OR 97217-3992
(503) 240-9346

South Carolina

U.S. Coast Guard, Marine Safety Office (REC)
196 Tradd Street
Charleston, SC 29401-1899
(843) 724-7693

Tennessee

U.S. Coast Guard, Marine Safety Office (REC)
200 Jefferson Avenue, Suite 1302
Memphis, TN 38103-2300
(901) 544-3297

Texas

U.S. Coast Guard, Marine Safety Office (REC)
8876 Gulf Freeway, Suite 200
Houston, TX 77017-6595
(713) 948-3350/51

Virginia

U.S. Coast Guard, Marine Safety Office (REC)
Norfolk Federal Bldg.
200 Granby Street, Suite 700
Norfolk, VA 23510-1888
(757) 441-3260

Washington

U.S. Coast Guard, Marine Safety Office (REC)
1519 Alaskan Way S.
Seattle, WA 98134-1192
(206) 217-6115

Guam

U.S. Coast Guard, Marine Safety Office (REC)
1026 Cabras Hwy., Suite 102
Piti, Guam 96910

Puerto Rico

U.S. Coast Guard, Marine Safety Office (REC)
P.O. Box 5-36'66
Old San Juan, PR 00902-3666
(787) 706-2400